2ZY

—— TO ——

NBH

An informal history
of the BBC in Manchester
and the North West

IAN HARTLEY

Willow
PUBLISHING

WILLOW PUBLISHING
Willow Cottage, 36 Moss Lane,
Timperley, Altrincham,
Cheshire, WA15 6SZ

First published 1987.

Printed in Great Britain by
The Commercial Centre Ltd.,
Clowes Street, Hollinwood, Oldham.

ISBN 0 946361 23 1

2ZY to NBH?

*The first BBC transmitter in
Manchester had the call sign 2ZY.
This book traces the development of
broadcasting from the very beginning
to the completion of New Broadcasting
House (NBH) as the BBC's
headquarters in the North of England.*

Contents

Acknowledgements

As an outsider looking in on the BBC I have relied a good deal on the memories of those in broadcasting and sincere thanks are due.

I am especially indebted to John Ithell at New Broadcasting House, Manchester for his support and for numerous introductions, and to Bernice Coupe in the BBC library. Thanks also to Neil Somerville and the staff at the BBC Written Archives at Caversham Park, Reading.

Dr. Peter Dawson at Micanite and Insulators Ltd. (G.E.C.) in Trafford Park was kind enough to allow me access to the records of 2ZY and I am indebted to the company for allowing reproduction of several photographs. Information was gratefully received from Pat Leggatt, former Head of BBC Engineering Information, Ray Webb Peter Batson, and David Hulme at Radio Manchester.

I am grateful to Basil H. Vernon, Hubert Taylor, Brian Trueman, Herbert Smith, Olive Shapley, Johnny Roadhouse, Joe Gladwin, Allan Shaw, Nick Hunter and Barney Colehan for their reminiscences and the numerous readers of the Manchester Evening News who responded to an article on my researches.

Introduction

An engrossing story of the wireless down the years that's compulsive reading for all who care about the integrity of Northern broadcasting.

The roll call of performers from Olive Shapley, Barney Colehan and Wilfred Pickles to Mike Harding, Ken Dodd, Les Dawson and the Grumbleweeds, encompasses all that is warm, affectionate, sometimes iconoclastic, sometimes erratically brilliant . . . but always consummately professional. I grew up under the aegis of Bob Stead, Tom Naisby, Graham Miller, John Tisdell, Bill Grundy and the great maestro Barney Colehan.

The quality of the spoken word was paramount. The nuances of our beautiful English language taught from the first flickerings of the green light. Integrity, honesty, warmth abounded in those far off days.

The B.B.C. was frequented by gentlemen. They stood out from their fellow men. I cherish the memories evoked by this professionally presented little tome.

STUART HALL

A. P. M. Fleming. *In charge of research at Metropolitan Vickers.*

K. A. Wright. *First pianist and station manager at 2ZY.*

Fleming, like Reith, was particularly interested in the social applications of broadcasting and set a standard for Wright to achieve. Wright's comment many years later was, 'How did we do it!?'

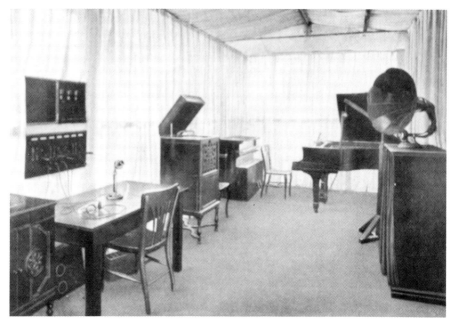

The 2ZY Studio. *Announcers, trios, dance bands and even a full military brass band could be packed into the 30ft × 16 ft converted conference room – and enjoyed it!*

Chapter One

THE PIONEERS

It was in 1899 that inventor, manufacturer and industrialist George Westinghouse bought 130 acres of Waters Meeting Farm on the Bridgewater Canal from the Trafford Park Estates. The land had been previously purchased by financier E. T. Hooley from Sir Humphrey de Trafford three years earlier and it was he who agreed to allow the Trafford Park to be converted from parkland into an industrial trading estate. Westinghouse built a huge factory of 11,000,000 bricks, 9,000,000 feet of timber and 17,000 tons of steel and within two years the factory was opened by the Lord Mayor of Manchester. The workforce soon were set to work making numerous electrical and mechanical engineering projects.

The company was known as British Westinghouse and soon became a truly British financed operation when the Metropolitan Carriage, Wagon and Finance Company provided funds to buy the American shareholdings in 1917. Two years later the company was taken over by Vickers Limited and became known as the Metropolitan Vickers Electrical Company, known first locally and then nationally as 'Metrovicks' or simply 'Metros'.

As the works neared completion in 1900 a young man joined the company to work in what was to be the research department. A. P. M. Fleming was thus in at the birth of the factory and before the main building was completed he and his colleagues set to work insulation testing and investigating transformer steels. He later became superintendent of the transformer department and during the war was also involved in the Lancashire Anti-Submarine Committee. It was after the war that his research department looked into a new phenomenon which had come into prominence during the war, namely telecommunications, and his thoughts turned to the possibility of beginning 'broadcasting' in Britain.

The American Westinghouse Company had been sending out regular programmes of music and speech from their East Pittsburgh station KDKA since December 1920 and the new craze had rapidly developed in America, so much so that by 1922 some 500 stations had been established. British amateurs were pressurising the Post Office to take a more liberal approach to licensing and

Metropolitan Vickers was one of the British firms then taking an active interest in the science.

Hugh Bell, one of the early engineers to work on the Manchester station went to America, and in 1920 was able to experience at first hand the public reaction to the KDKA broadcasts. He soon passed this information on to Fleming who visited the United States the following year. Fleming saw for himself the ethereal chaos of 500 stations feverishly competing with each other, often with similar frequencies and with little or no liaison. He looked at all aspects of broadcasting, both technical and cultural, and his report back to the Metrovick board makes interesting reading with numerous comments on the programmes' contents. For him there was too much jazz and popular music and 'good classical programmes were few and far between. In fact the only programmes that would appeal to a thoroughly musical European would appear to be the operatic transmissions given by land line as at Chicago'. He decided that, 'musical programmes should be carefully segregated into distinct types so that the public would know beforehand on which nights to expect programmes to suit their tastes'. He had already had the idea to use the Halle Orchestra by broadcasting concerts from the Free Trade Hall, which he thought would have 'very wide appeal'. As Reith was to do in London, so Fleming set the tone and quality of the broadcasting content in Manchester. By his return from America, Fleming was committed to an attempt to initiate a broadcasting service in Manchester.

Manchester already had a Wireless Society with many enthusiastic amateurs transmitting to each other and eager to support any new venture into broadcasting. Metros were primarily manufacturers of heavy equipment and had little experience of wireless components, but Captain R. S. Hilton, managing director at Metros, was also a director of the Radio Communication Company of Slough, a company engaged in the marine radio equipment. It seemed appropriate that R.C.C. should supply the apparatus to set up the Manchester station and assist with its development, and the co-operation between the two companies would provide substantial competition to the Marconi Company rapidly developing its broadcasting prowess in the south.

For R.C.C. Basil Binyon liaised with Fleming over the new venture and the two went to see F. J. Brown at the Post Office to gather the authority's views on the enterprise. They had prepared their case well, and stressed the educational and cultural benefits from their scheme. They assured Brown that it was 'not a blatant advertising scheme'. The following day, March 31st, Fleming wrote formally to the Postmaster General asking for a licence to establish two broadcasting stations, one in Manchester and the other in Slough. In his letter he asked to be able to broadcast from 4 to 5 am and from 7.30 to 10 pm on weekdays, but would reduce these hours on Sundays 'in order to suit the public demand for church services or special music' and again stressed the public service aspect, remarking that the company would work to the 'best public interest'.

Much confusion existed over the patent situation with the Marconi Company, which was to prove troublesome for all those firms then taking an interest in broadcasting. Nevertheless, the Metros' team began experimenting with a small transmitter in Hale. This was erected at 'Highclere', Fleming's house, some six miles away from the factory and it had the call sign 2WH. A single phase induction motor on the Altrincham electrical supply drove the 1500 volt generator at 1500 rpm to be used as an 'exciter'. A 150 ft aerial was erected, 75 ft high and with a 12 ft spread. Trials mostly of gramophone records began early in 1922, while studio space was being found at the factory.

Metrovicks had an old iron water tower which was a landmark in the area and an ideal spot on which to hang a transmitting aerial. Luckily this tower was close to the research building and the research conference room was commandeered for the purpose of a studio. Under the stairs next to the conference room was a small area which could be used to contain the transmitter and the initial 60 watt version was constructed there. Looking today at the space afforded those early engineers, one can only marvel at how not only equipment, but sometimes several staff, worked in those cramped conditions. A 200 ft aerial was strung between the tower and the gable end of the main factory building and a lead taken down into the transmitter room. This first aerial proved too long and an 80 ft version was inserted into the middle of the original span. Later this single line was substituted with six wires, each of 3 ft loops forming a 'cage' aerial.

The studio measured 30 ft by 16 ft. A wooden frame about 2 ft from the walls was constructed and onto this was draped fine sailcloth in an attempt to create good acoustic conditions. Heavy velure curtaining was also used on both ceiling and walls and the floor was covered with half-inch thick felt. There was little experience in the field of acoustics and the studios were made far too 'dead', causing a claustrophobic atmosphere and putting off many artists who relied on some resonance to aid their performance. The room was described at the time as 'spacious'. Other than the very occasional 'outside broadcast', all transmissions came from this one room.

Because the engineers could not see or hear the performers in the studio, other than what was going out on the air, a 'control box' was fitted in the studio so that directions could be given to the 'studio manager' – a title given to anyone not actually performing in the studio at the time. A display of 15 pilot lights enabled the engineer to signal to the studio such instructions as 'O.K.', 'Microphone', 'Backwards', 'Louder', 'Keep Steady' or, with monotonous regularity, 'Close Down'. The announcer or manager would acknowledge receipt of the information by means of a single pilot light, or so was the theory.

Much discussion went on as to whether to use the R.C.C. method of modulation as the Marconi patents' availability was obscure, but all tests 'pointed to the superiority of the choke control for simplicity and stability' and eventually this was used. The electronic stage was thus set for both artist and audience to make of it what they could.

2ZY Aerial. *The water tower at Metrovicks provided an ideal anchor for the transmitter aerial, which was suspended between the tower and the highest point of the main building. The tower was demolished in the war to prevent its being used as a landmark.*

Chapter Two

2ZY CALLING

The first programme broadcast from the Metrovick station was on 17 May, 1922.

PROGRAMME

1. Extract from the 'Times'. Friday, May 12th.
    Speech by Mr. Mckenna.
    Wavelength 450 metres.

2. (Gramophone) – Violin Solo.
    'Berceuse' (Townsend) played by Fritz Kreisler.
    Wavelength 400 metres.

3. (Gramophone) – Soprano.
    'Sempre libera gedd'io folleggaire' sung by Amelia Galli-Curci.
    Wavelength 425 metres.

4. Extract from German Newspaper (Neue Freie Presse).
    Description of Lloyd George at his house at Genoa.
    Wavelength 425 metres.

5. (Gramophone) – Fox Trot.
    'Why, Dear' played by Joseph C. Smith's Orchestra.
    Wavelength 450 metres.

The Manchester Evening Chronicle (price 1d) gave it a single column story with the headline 'City Wireless Tonight' giving a run-down of the programmes. After that they failed to give further details of broadcasts for quite some time.

Further broadcasts were made during the following months, all carefully monitored at Fleming's home in Hale. Each item was listed and technical notes, as well as comments on quality of reception and performance, were made. During the period of these experimental broadcasts, no payment was made to performers and virtually all programmes were made by Metrovick staff working often outside their normal hours, and 'it was necessary for the organiser not only to arrange his programmes, but also to tempt his staff'!

The Post Office was in discussion with several interested groups as to the future structuring of broadcasting in Britain and eventually it was agreed to grant a two year licence to the British Broadcasting Company to be formed by six large firms, namely British Thomson–Houston Company (BTH), General Electric Company (GEC), Marconi, Metropolitan Vickers, Radio Communications Company (RCC) and Western Electric, along with numerous smaller companies. A. McKinstrey was the Metrovick representative and signed the historic licensing document for the company on 15 December, 1922.

Much technical development had gone on in Manchester, and a 700 watt transmitter had been ordered from R.C.C. back in October when it appeared that a licence might be granted. Within two weeks a transmitter was installed and tested for the first time on 25 October. To be on the safe side, the station in Fleming's home was upgraded to 200 watts in case there was any failure at Trafford Park. The nearby aircraft station, 'Gem', which used a very nonselective receiver, forced the transmitter at Trafford Park to be used during night hours only so as not to interfere with aircraft signals. It had been agreed that during the experimental period, the station would cease to broadcast at regular intervals to listen for SOS messages, and programmes were regularly interrupted with the phrase 'We are now closing down for three minutes'.

From 22 July, broadcasts were made weekly and soon more frequently, the early transmissions being mainly records. Soon there were discussions on general topics and special programmes for children. In fact the station claimed to be the first in Britain to offer children's programmes and to coin the term 'auntie' for their presenters. On his trip to America, Fleming had noted the popularity of 'Children's Bedtime Stories', a feature on many American wireless stations, and had suggested this as a suitable idea for the Manchester Experimental Station.

One of the great problems was not so much the working of the transmitter and generator, frought though this was with teething troubles, but the quality of the sound from the studio. It had been noticed on early test broadcasts that a standard carbon microphone, though just about adequate for speech, left much to be desired when used for music, especially the piano. Microphone development was thus essential. Several methods were devised using the modulation of a light source onto a photosensitive cell. One used an acetylene flame as the light source, which was modulated by a diaphragm. This was bulky and immobile, and there were many cries of 'keep that b..... door shut!' as the slightest gust of air could cause a flicker of the flame with disastrous results. The final development of the photophone provided a pencil-thin beam of light onto a selenium cell, and even gramophone pickups were

2ZY Transmitter. *The transmitter was located under a staircase. After a particularly expressive glissando from a trombone directly into the microphone there was an enormous flash from under the stairs and all the lights went out. As the door opened Basil Vernon emerged from the smoke and moaned, 'Now you've done it. You've gone and busted the bloody valve!' (K. A. Wright)*

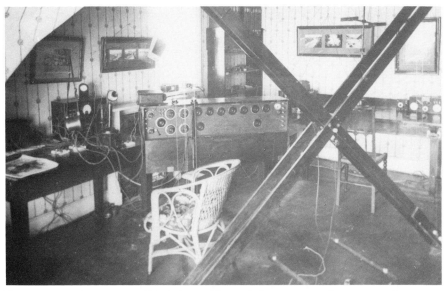

Transmitter/Receiver at Highclere. *Fleming's home was used to monitor the station's output and as a back-up transmitter 'just in case'.*

modified to utilise this arrangement.

The horn into which the performer had to speak or sing, had to be kept perfectly rigid and it was the height of the performer which was adjusted rather than that of the microphone. This was often achieved with copies of the Encyclopaedia Britannica. One exceptionally short tenor had to be provided with quite a bundle of books, and as he reached for his final crescendo, oblivious of his predicament, he stepped backward and the piece of music came to an abrupt halt.

Due to an inherent resonance and lack of portability, the 'photophone' system had little potential and new ideas were needed. Piezo crystals were tried but proved only satisfactory on the gramophone. One of the best reproductions was achieved when the coil and magnet from an Amplion loudspeaker was used and, after careful damping with first oil and then vaseline, this apparatus came to be used regularly. Also developed simultaneously in London, the system became known as the magnetophone.

The team at Trafford Park was only given 24 hours notice that they were to begin official broadcasting. Those 24 hours were hectic. The station had already gathered together a group of enthusiasts and these, along with the official staff, put together the first night's broadcasting on 15 November 1922, just a day after 2LO had started regular broadcasting in London. The transmission began '2ZY calling, 2ZY calling. Our transmission tonight will consist of late news followed by musical items. At 7 pm we shall send a short story to children, followed by music after which election results will be transmitted up to 11 pm'.

On that first evening Miss A. Bennie presented the first 'Kiddies Corner' with Kenneth A. Wright, who became the first station manager in Manchester at the early age of 22. Miss Bennie was known as the 'Lady of the Magic Carpet' and she told the Oscar Wilde story of 'The Happy Prince'. She taught English at the girls' English classes, which were held in the works, and chose to read a story rather than make up one as she had done on other occasions, as she said she was 'much too scared to trust my powers as a storyteller before the microphone'. She wrote later: 'After I had done my stunt, I remember I hurried home to listen in on a crystal set, which we had got for the occasion and, as we lived some 17 miles away from Trafford Park, we had some misgivings as to whether we should get anything. However, we were fortunate and heard everything splendidly'. Kenneth Wright, who became well known to children in the North as Uncle Humpty Dumpty, presented some recorded music for the children as he did on numerous subsequent nights. The General Election, results of which were broadcast that night, brought Bonar Law to power. The election was a useful coincidence, demonstrating the immediacy of the news broadcasting of radio and giving a few newspaper proprietors sleepless nights. H. G. Bell as Mr. X told humorous stories, and records of dance music continued until closedown at 1.15 am.

From that first official broadcast until the move from Trafford Park, the 'Kiddies Corner' was presented three or four times each week. Other members of staff who enjoyed working on the children's programmes were Mr. S. J. Nightingale as 'The Sandman', Miss A. L. Bennie known as 'Cousin Bunny' and Miss J. M. Cormack who became 'The Cloud Lady'. Even in those very early days, many letters were received from appreciative children who often sent in their photographs, many of the children listening with rapt attention to broadcasts through their headphones. Miss A. Bennie wrote that the looks of appreciation were 'ample reward for the voluntary overtime that those early days involved'.

Here are a few examples of letters received:

'My youngest sister Margaret, aged 7, has been ill in bed this week and one of the things which has helped her has been looking forward for the stories told every evening.'
Lulu, 3 December, 1922.

'I should like particularly to express my appreciation of Uncle Humpty Dumpty's efforts on behalf of the kiddies. I may say that judging from reports which I receive from all quarters he has already become an institution with the children . . . .'
Timperley, Cheshire. 5 December, 1922.

'Uncle Humpty Dumpty is most queer
He's like an egg from ear to ear,
His life must be rather bitter
As he has to talk down a transmitter.

I'm always sorry when he bids us 'Good-night',
But it's best to be jolly and bright.
And I like the music he plays
For it always fits in whatever he says.'
Hilda. 5 December, 1922.

As well as music and stories there were talks on nature, industry and gardening, as well as fashion notes and seasonal recipes. These were all provided by members of the staff of the research department, with just a few notable guests such as Sybil Thorndyke who talked to the children on 24 April, 1923. Music was provided by various 'artists' from the Metrovick staff, most regularly by Jessie Cormack on piano.

The studio had a Steinway 'baby grand' piano and a Steinway Welte reproducing (pianola) piano, both loaned free of charge from Steinway, London. Records could be played on the New Edison Diamond Disc Phonograph or an Aeolian Vocalation Graduola Cabinet Gramophone, loaned free from E. S. Wright and Sons Ltd., Manchester. With both musical and written material, little regard was taken of copyright.

Programming for adults also consisted of talks (often slotted into Mr. X's Corner), musical interludes, news and the occasional play. Lawrence du Garde Peach, who visited the Trafford Park station in 1922 and was persuaded to tell stories and sing that same visit, was so impressed by the new medium that he wrote the first play ever to be broadcast in Britain, called 'Light and Shade'. A typical evening's entertainment is shown below:–

15

FRIDAY, 15 DECEMBER, 1922.

4.00   Call up.
'Uncle Humpty Dumpty' with the Fairy Swan Music.

4.10   News Bulletin.

4.15   Song. 'Oh, Why So Long Delaying?' from Mozart's 'Le Nozze di Figaro', by Maria Barrientos.

4.20   Song. 'It Was A Lover and His Lass'. (Eric Coates) sung by Sydney J. Nightingale.

4.25   Violin Solo. 'Meditation' (Massenet) by Mischa Elman.

4.30   Announcements. Goodbye.

5.55   Call up. Announcements.

6.00   Story and music for younger children by 'The Lady of the Magic Carpet'.

6.15   Late News from Reuter and other News Agencies.

6.30   Story and music for older children by 'Uncle Humpty Dumpty' and 'The Lady of the Magic Carpet'.

6.50   Transmission of the first part of Tschaikowski's 'Nut-Cracker Suite' by Steinway Welte reproducing piano.

7.30   Mr. X's Corner.

8.00   Concert by members of St. John's Prize Choir, Weast, conducted by John T. Edwards.

9.15   Special Late News from Reuter and other News Agencies.

9.30   Dance Music.

10.00   Musical Programmes.

10.30   Second programme of Dance Music.

11.00   Final Announcements. 'Goodnight.'

Music was to form a great deal of those early broadcasts, relying to a great extent on gramophone records. Basil Binyon wrote to McInstrey in November 1923 and commented that he thought that 2ZY was relying too much on records which 2LO and the Birmingham station 5IT did not use to the same extent. Hawaian music was one of the favourites with both audience and engineers, as the staccato twanging style did not appear as distorted over the air. The first 'live' musical item had been provided by Mr. E. B. Bell when on 25 December he performed the 'Hallelujah Chorus' and Wagner's 'Pilgrims Chorus' on the concertina! K. E. Wright was perhaps the first station pianist and Douglas Black, who was able to co-opt many friends and relatives to perform, could be classed as the first unofficial orchestra leader. Some of the 'Hale' notes were far from complementary about those early musical items. One noted that a piano piece sounded as though it was played 'on a banjo'.

In April 1923, P. P. Eckersley, the B.B.C.'s Chief Engineer, wrote to Arthur Fleming and said that 'though he was not trying to run down the Manchester station in any way' and though he thought Manchester was working under difficult conditions, yet he did feel that, comparing reception reports, Manchester was of variable quality. In Manchester N. P. Hinton, Chief Radio Engineer, J. W. Buckley of Metrovick Research and N. Lea, the Chief Engineer of R.C.C., refuted claims that their wavelength was not constant and Fleming sent a copy of a congratulatory letter he had received, to Eckersley, who commented he would be 'happier if he had 200 of the same'. Nevertheless, the Manchester station was being received far afield: –

'We are pleased to announce the excellence of the wireless concerts transmitted from your station. The singing and music is quite clear and the clarity of tone is excellent.'
Newry, County Down, Ulster. 9 December, 1922.

'I cannot help but write telling you the pleasure that your wireless concerts have given to my father and mother, who are both 76 years of age.'
Liverpool. 29 November, 1922.

'If this is a specimen of what we are to receive in English Broadcasting I think that we have every reason to congratulate ourselves on our good luck.'
Taunton. 30 October, 1922.

Metrovicks, concurrent with developing the transmitter, were also actively designing receivers, for it was this side of broadcasting where their profits, they hoped, would lie. Both 'cat's whisker' and valve sets were designed, and by the autumn of 1922 they were ready to launch an advertising campaign for their crystal 'Radiophone' set selling at £4.10s. Valve 'Radiophones' soon followed. In 1923 a modular system was launched for the enthusiast. These were the 'Radiobrix', a series of numbered units in standard cubes, such as an h.f. amplifier or an l.f. amplifier, and with these the amateur could construct his own receiver from crystal set to six valve set. In 1924 the Cosmos Shortpath Valve began to be marketed and the Cosmos trademark initiated.

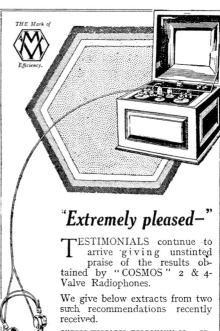

Local companies began to specialise in the wireless business

Major companies involved in broadcasting established branches in Manchester and several small businesses added to their stock in trade by selling wireless components, and some began commercially making components and sets. Webson (Manchester) Limited was one such company which competed with the major wireless manufacturers. John Webb had undertaken several inventive ways of supporting his family in Didsbury, and after the first world war began machining parts for crystal sets in his premises at No. 1 King Street (now Kings Lynn Close) Didsbury. He also offered a service recharging accumulators from the 200 volt DC supply. Voltage adjustment was done by the inclusion in the circuit of different numbers of carbon lamps dependent on the number of batteries to be charged. He also had premises at 35 Claremont Grove and there manufactured his own crystal set and later valve sets. Speakers too were made on the premises, the frames of which were cast, the coils hand turned and the cones hand made from Whatman drawing paper with a wash leather surround. The company was BBC approved, displaying the emblem on their sets.

Wireless construction, until 1922 only attempted by the real enthusiast, was now becoming commonplace. Youngsters saved up their pocket money to buy components and followed instructions published in magazines like 'Wireless World' and 'Popular Wireless'. When the 'tuner' had been constructed by wrapping wires round pieces of cardboard, the crystal secured and the headphones connected, then came the task of finding the station. The advantage of the self-contained unit soon became obvious to youngsters who could secrete the apparatus under their bed in order to drop off to sleep listening to the Savoy Orpheans, one of the most popular broadcasting bands in the twenties. Before the programmes began one could tune onto the 'carrier wave', this signal being like 'the sound of rushing water'. Some schoolteachers with experience in telegraphy or an interest in electronics showed their pupils short cuts in construction, such as using an enamelled copper wire wrapped round a 'Panshine' tube, a spring plunger from an electric lamp-holder, and a galena crystal to construct a wireless set in school. The aerial might be stretched over the playground and the excited children were then able to listen to the announcers on 2ZY.

One of those early announcers was Victor Smythe who arrived in Trafford Park one wet day in February 1923 without notice, resplendent in 'wide brimmed hat and a long, fur-collared coat suggestive of Henry Irving'. Smythe did a comic turn called Algy's Priceless Piffle and was so successful that it became a regular Saturday night feature. He had been in the film industry, concert parties and the legitimate theatre. He was badly wounded at Arras and was hospitalised for two and a half years and was then looking for a job in broadcasting. He helped to arrange 'stunts' and other features at Trafford Park, and along with A. E. Grimshaw and D. H. Clarke, became a regular announcer. He would often work from 10 am to the early hours of the next morning, and once undraped and removed the whole studio between midday and 5 am. It is said that after one particularly tiring day, Smythe not only gave his customary 'Good night everybody, go–o–o–od night', but added to the engineer 'Pull that bloody switch out', a remark that scandalised many listeners. Such 'faux-pas'

19

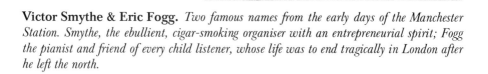

Victor Smythe & Eric Fogg. *Two famous names from the early days of the Manchester Station. Smythe, the ebullient, cigar-smoking organiser with an entrepreneurial spirit; Fogg the pianist and friend of every child listener, whose life was to end tragically in London after he left the north.*

did not halt his career, however, and he took over his official duties when the experimental station moved to Dickinson Street in 1923.

The experimental station soon formed its own trio of Jessie Cormack (piano), Sidney Wright (cello) and Leonard Hirsch (violin), who was first spotted by Kenneth Wright playing in the Brooks Bar Picture House. Wright spent half a day each week auditioning entertainers in a large room at Forsyth's in Deansgate. As well as Station Manager, Wright described himself: 'not only was I newsreader and announcer, but also accompanyist, programme planner, and general bottle-washer'. He even distributed 100 of the latest crystal sets so that locals could listen to a selection of the Mikado, first dubbed several times from the pianola onto a Dictaphone cylinder 'to save my aching feet'.

One night whilst reading the news, Wright received a note saying that his tailor, Mr. Bunny, could not give a talk due in a few minutes. It was to be on 'Coming Fashions'. Wright knew nothing of the subject and his mind was on other matters. Nevertheless, he attempted to read the talk himself. A slip of the tongue caused him to say 'shirts' instead of 'skirts' and laughter from the transmitting room stopped him in his tracks. The next day a newspaper headline read 'Shirts will Be Shorter, Says Wireless'. According to Wright, Reith was not amused.

Many artists became regular broadcasters and one notable achievement was when blind pianist Edward Isaacs went over to Paris to broadcast a recital from the Eiffel Tower. Manchester tried to pick up this signal and relay it from the 2ZY transmitter. The receiver and transmitter were so close together that Mr. Basil Harcourt Vernon, one of the engineers, felt sure that listeners would only hear a 'big howl' of feedback, as Trafford Park picked up its own signal. However, all went well with this momentous broadcast and inspired further relay attempts. The Eiffel Tower time signals were often broadcast. The station had earlier had an ingenious method of relaying the sound of Big Ben. The Metrovick offices in London were close to the Houses of Parliament and one of the staff put a phone call through to Manchester just before the 'hour' and held the telephone microphone outside the window. The signal was then transmitted from Manchester. Later, in Liverpool, Basil Vernon placed microphones in the Church of St. Paul's so that the Liverpool station could use the chimes as time signals. Possibly the greatest relay the Manchester station achieved, was the rebroadcasting of signals received at the Hale station from KDKA at Pittsburg. So already, in 1923, the Manchester public could listen to live programmes from across the Atlantic.

Basil Vernon was one of the two Metrovick staff seconded to the BBC at Trafford Park and went on to have a long distinguished career with the BBC, becoming Chief Engineer in the North. He was involved with the first outside broadcast that 2ZY attempted. This was from the Oxford Cinema, Manchester, where the young pianist, Eric Fogg, was spotted by Wright playing for the silent films. The GPO connected a telephone cable between the cinema and the studio, and Mr. Vernon with a colleague went along to the cinema with microphone and other equipment they had made themselves, and Mr. Fogg gave the first of thousands of broadcasts for the BBC. He then went under the strange nom-de-plume of 'Keyboard Kitty' but later, as Uncle Eric, became one of Manchester's most loved 'uncles'.

21

Isobel Baillie (right) and musicians broadcasting from Trafford Park. *She was a regular broadcaster and starred in the first show from the station. She later recalled, 'One was not really conscious of being present at a moment of history. Although one was jolly excited, one was never quite sure who might be listening.'*

One of the most famous regular musical broadcasters from Trafford Park was Isobel (later Dame Isobel) Baillie. Bella, as she was known to her friends, sang ballads, usually accompanied by violin and piano. The studio was very handy for her as she lived close by in Stretford and so 2ZY was lucky to use her services at a time when she was beginning her successful career. She was born on 9 March, 1895 and had sung for many years locally when she ventured into a professional career in 1922. For over thirty years she was one of England's finest singers of oratorio.

Attempts were made to broadcast orchestras as outside broadcasts and from the studio. Shorrocks Dance Band and the Oxford Picture House Orchestra were regularly heard and for the most part transmissions went well. However, one visit to the studio by the Band of the Grenadier Guards, caused great problems. The studio staff were told two days before that the whole band would be broadcasting and to make arrangements. For a day and a night, the engineers laboured to build a temporary studio in the Trafford Park Works' Social Club, some distance from the cramped studio. All was ready for the band's arrival. But, try as they may, the engineers could not achieve a sound link with the transmitter. Half an hour before the broadcast, the band had to pack up their instruments and treck back to the original studio. Quickly the pianola, gramophone and other equipment were moved onto the roadway, windows were removed and the band arranged with the tuba and drums outside in the yard. All the way through the broadcast, the only access to the studio was through the window and engineers regularly squeezed through to adjust microphones and musicians. Everyone was glad when the programme was over, especially Victor Smythe, who as announcer was perched on the window-sill throughout the broadcast! Nevertheless, the station was inundated with congratulatory letters and requests for more.

The visit of a beauty queen to the station one day almost stopped broadcasting. Engineers coming in from the transmitter room to complain that nothing was going out over the air, found the studio deserted. All the staff had offered to take the lady for a drink and eventually one poor soul was found to play records and give repeated weather forecasts until the others returned. The atmosphere at the station in those days was, to say the least, informal. Comedy was in the hands of local artists like Foden Williams or occasional visiting stars like Stanley Holloway and Dave Burnaby who appeared on an uproarious Children's Hour. A few weeks later Harry Tate visited the station. Members of the Metrovick staff, J. W. Buckley and R. T. Fleming, performed humorous sketches as Rastus and Massa Johnson.

Chapter Three

GOING
TO TOWN

The Metrovick station continued to function for the BBC officially until July 1923, but unofficially into August. In July the new Dickinson Street station was to open in the centre of Manchester, but the team at Trafford Park was asked to stand-by in case of hitches. Sure enough, on that opening day there was a snag with the new transmitter and Trafford Park continued to send out signals, a fact that was not public knowledge at the time. The new studios were opened in the presence of Lord Gainsford, J. C. W. Reith and Sir William Noble, who all spoke. The band of the Irish Guards played, and Florence Holding and Lee Thistlethwaite sang.

Some of the old team transferred to 57 Dickinson Street, with the flamboyant Victor Smythe having gathered much experience at Metrovicks, initially becoming the mainstay in the studio as senior presenter. He often broadcast wearing a monocle and became one of the great characters of the station. Some, but not all, of the engineering staff, transferred employment from Metrovicks to the BBC and entertainers used at Trafford Park were called upon to continue in central Manchester. K. A. Wright married Jessie Cormack at St. Cuthbert's Church, Sheffield on Christmas Eve, 1923 and left the Manchester station for greater heights in London. In April 1924, he wrote to his old boss A. P. M. Fleming saying that 'the team spirit with which the station abounded in the old days, has entirely gone west'. He also commiserated with Fleming who, although in at the very beginning of broadcasting, had been somewhat left on the sidelines, which Wright thought unfair considering the tremendous amount of work he had done in the early days.

Dan Godfrey Jnr. became station director in August 1923 and also formed the 2ZY Orchestra. Music was Godfrey's first love and he determined to make the station renowned for this aspect of broadcasting. He had taken over a station, however, severely restricted for space, where access was either up 100 steps or by a hand-operated goods lift. This was the only lift in the building, and for visiting dignitaries was bedecked with a few curtains. The station was sited in the top storey of a warehouse close by Manchester Corporation Power Station, the chimneys of which were used to support the transmitting aerial. Because of the close proximity of the generators, there was a continuous 'hum' and the atmosphere was full of static. It was said that watches would gain up to half an hour each day because of this! The original 'earth' for the transmitter was achieved by throwing a forty feet long copper bar into the Bridgewater Canal, but this proved unsatisfactory. Eventually, wires were fixed to the base of the chimney radiating outwards. Residents of Stretford complained at the reduction in quality of reception but no effort was made to improve the transmitter and the complaints only stopped as listeners improved their receivers.

Sidney George Honey (Uncle George) was deputy Station Director at Dickinson Street and took over control of the children's programmes which featured Auntie Rosalind (Rhodes), Cousin Edward, Uncle Victor (Smythe), Uncle Willie (Cochrane) and Nephew Eric. Sidney Honey's talks to children on a wide variety of topics became so popular that when he resigned after a disagreement with head office in 1924, he agreed to continue his Sunday evening 'Talks for Young People' at 8 pm each week.

Following the suggestion of a young listener of the Birmingham Station in 1923, that a club for children listeners be formed, each station eventually set up its own 'Radio Circle'. These were run in conjunction with the Children's Hour, and the Manchester circle was particularly successful with over 15,000 members within the first few years. Members took on many charitable schemes, often collecting for wireless sets for children's wards in hospitals and for blind schools. Being a member one initially had the right to have one's birthday read over the air, but soon sheer numbers forced this to be abandoned except for special cases. The Manchester Station ran several excursions and entertainments for members and the Circles brought a close relationship between young listeners and their radio Aunts and Uncles.

One young entertainer, whose radio career was concentrated into the two and a half years at Dickinson Street, was Hubert Taylor, who at 13 years old played piano for the children's programmes, and provided the musical introduction and play out music for Sidney Honey's Sunday talks. Hubert, or Cousin Hubert as he became known, was an excellent pianist at that early age, and although he was given no payment for his children's programmes, raced to the studios each evening after school to entertain his fans. Many wrote to him and one which amused him said that his interpretation of Debussy's 'Golliwog Cake Walk', 'set my blood all tingling'. For the music which accompanied Honey's talks he was paid the princely sum of 10/6d for the introduction and 10/6d for the ending music. Honey did not seem to have much faith in the future of the wireless and advised the young Taylor that he should pursue a career in something more stable. Mr. Taylor did and eventually took over Manchester's 'Music Exchange', selling the music he had so brilliantly played.

Great strides were made in the improvement of programme presentation at Dickinson Street, and experiments both technical and cultural were made using local talent. All might not have been so, however. One Sunday afternoon the announcer's voice suddenly became urgent. It was Manchester's first radio SOS. 'Will Mister Dan Godfrey or Victor Smythe come to the studio at once – as it is on fire.' Dan Godfrey at his Buxton home, heard the message and rushed back to the studio. In the fire, musical instruments were destroyed but the fire brigade came in time to save the studio and transmitter.

Sydney Honey & Rosalind Rhodes. *Two of the broadcasters who took a special interest in programmes for children. Honey took on the direction of the early children's programmes at the Dickinson Street studios.*

Another 'disaster' which befell at about this time, was an invasion by Manchester students on their 'rag' day. It was probably the only occasion when the BBC was not in control of one of its stations. 'Mr. Godd Damfrey' conducted the '2ZY Broadblasting Orchestra' in what was to be a concert, but turned out tunes like 'Yes, We Have No Bananas'; a deep voiced Auntie Rosalind sent all her children a 'nice big, warm kiss', there was a metallic whirr followed by a resounding 'plop'; the weather forecast stated 'It will be the same as tomorrow' and a news item on a lady celebrating her 195th birthday said she had drunk gin all her life and could still crack a bottle open with her two remaining molars! The station eventually returned to normal after some hours of mayhem.

A whole range of musical and spoken entertainment was now undertaken at 2ZY. The station had its own chorus putting on operas such as Carmen and excellent concerts. On the educational front, Edward J. Whitnall BSc. gave a series of talks on animals, and a letter from Spain thanked the BBC for the talks in Spanish being given on the Manchester station by W. F. Bletcher. One regular, unusual item, was entitled 'Mr. Percy Phlage will percyflage'? It had been hoped that the move to the city centre would encourage more artists to 'appear' on radio, as some were put off by the trip to Trafford Park and this seemed to be working. The popularity of 'the wireless' was growing and even Tom Smith the 'cracker king' made a series of crackers with wireless novelties in them. One contained the verse: –

'From Manchester with anxious voice
Is asking you to make your choice.
Just a moment 2ZY
It needs a Y Z 2 reply.'

The public was beginning to accept the service as commonplace. One day a woman rushed into the Manchester station and demanded to see the Director as a matter of urgency. She had missed the train to Blackpool and wanted an announcement made to tell those waiting of her situation so that they wouldn't miss their tea.

Belle Vue Zoo asked if the station would broadcast that they had lost a flamingo and asked the public to look out for it. The station soon got a phone call from someone who had found a bird with the same description, but strange to relate, it was another flamingo! Even the authorities were warming to the new medium and in a letter from Sir Robert Peacock, the then Chief Constable of Manchester, he expressed his appreciation of services rendered to the police by broadcasting, especially in two instances where the owner of premises on fire had been contacted, and a witness to a fatal accident came forward after an appeal.

The BBC at that time believed that having an official who could also appear in programmes was most cost effective. This proved to be false economy in many cases. Godfrey turned out to be a better musician than an administrator and eventually was moved to London where he became Musical Director of the 2LO Wireless Orchestra in 1924.

In May 1924, Basil E. Nichols (later Sir Basil) was appointed as the new Director.

He had graduated from Oxford and been an administrator in India previously. T. H. Morrison, who had been leader of the Opera House Orchestra, took over from Dan Godfrey musically, becoming the Director of Music. In June a new company was set up called 'The Planets' in order to produce comedy plays during the summer. Each actor took the name of a planet and audiences were invited to guess their identities. The listener with the nearest correct solution was invited to spend an evening in the studio while the programmes were in progress. In September, the Halle Orchestra broadcasts began under the direction of their conductor, Sir Hamilton Harty. These were to become a regular and popular item.

The Halle concerts and other outside broadcasts were the technical responsibility of Messrs. Florence, Wood, Vernon, Payne, Williams and Fleming, the station's engineers, and these were becoming more and more commonplace. Most, like the community singing from Houldsworth Hall, Deansgate, went according to plan, but on one occasion when the connection to the studio announcer was lost, a concert was broadcast without any announcements between items. The public, however, liked the lack of announcer and wrote to say so. Continuous concerts thus became quite common.

Not all correspondence was in praise of the station. Mrs. D. Patterson of Bowdon wrote to complain of the 'patronising tone' of the speakers; that she thought there should be more of the Halle concerts; and asked why the speech given by the Prince of Wales had not been broadcast as it had on other stations, and there had been instead a zoo programme.

B. E. Nichols replied that he would look into the patronising tone complaint (one that was levelled at many station announcers – especially on children's programmes in the early years). The complaint as to the length of Halle concerts was a reasonable one as, because of an agreement that had been made with the Halle Orchestra, only one hour of any concert could be broadcast and this had to be strictly adhered to – so much so that often the programme stopped in the middle of a piece of music. It was not long before a more sensible arrangement was reached. As to the last item on the lady's complaint list – the broadcast of the Prince of Wales had apparently only been 'offered' to some stations to transmit, as 'simultaneous broadcasting' was still in its infancy. The lack of any recording system meant that once such a broadcast had been given it could never be 'saved' for other stations.

In his final paragraph to Miss Patterson, Nichols spelt out the dilemma with which many of his contemporaries were struggling – that of the balance of programme content, and how the BBC had to try to broadcast the best in music and yet had to attract a large audience. They could not be too elitist, as at that time listeners had only one station to which they could listen.

Some complaints, maybe due to poor reception, were totally unjustified. One lady, for example, phoned irately to say that she thought swearing, especially on children's programmes, was inexcusable. She said she had heard the storyteller say that night's item was 'a hell of a story'. In fact the announcer said that 'tonight there is an elephant story'!

B. E. Nichols was offered a position in London in 1925 and yet another joined

Badges of the Radio Circle issued by the Manchester Station. *The upper two were unique to 2ZY, but soon a standard design was issued based on the Cardiff and Swansea circle's badge. This is the lowest of the three showing the attachment for the North Region. Being a member entitled one to have birthdays announced on the air, but the popularity of the circles soon made this impractical and the last birthdays were announced in 1933. Good works stimulated by the example of the Radio circles continued however almost up to the end of Children's Hour in 1964.*

"AUNTIES AND UNCLES" FROM 2 ZY.

Front Row: Cousin Tom, Cousin Peg, Uncle Willie, Auntie Rosalind, Uncle Ronald, Aunt Jean, Cousin Helen.
Middle Row: Cousin Doris, Cousin Gwen, Uncle Don, Uncle Pat, Uncle Eric, Fairy Godmother, Cousin Bernard, Cousin Fred.
Back Row: Cousin Mac, Cousin Hilda, Uncle Sydney, Alice-in-Wonderland, Uncle Billy, Cousin Clare.

THE KIDDIES' HOUR.

"Aunts" and "Uncles" to Stay at 2ZY.

The B.B.C. has decided that the "Aunts" and "Uncles" who have been familiar to tiny—and big—listeners during the Children's Hour, shall no longer figure as such in the programme.

An official stated to-day that the scope of the Children's Hour is being extended.

"We are," he said, "bringing in more outside people to broadcast, and it was thought to be invidious for some to be called 'aunts' and 'uncles.'"

Mr. E. Liveing, station director of 2ZY, said that though the "Aunts" and "Uncles" have been retained in the Children's Hour at Manchester, a good deal of reorganisation has taken place in connection with this feature.

"The changes have only been brought about after the most careful consideration," he said. "A good deal of the back-chat' between those taking part in the Children's Hour has been cut out, and a very definite programme arranged for each day.

"Every effort is being made to keep the Children's Hour light and bright, but it is felt advisable to give something that will definitely benefit the young listeners' tastes in regard to literature and music."

The Children's Hour was probably the most popular programme and sometimes the least planned. Eventually the 'Hour' became better planned and even rehearsed! (Article from the Manchester Guardian, 8 January, 1927.)

the exodus of talent from the North. He took up duties in Schools' Broadcasting, an area of broadcasting he had pioneered in Manchester. In the spring of 1924, experimental lessons and talks were broadcast. A local committee had been set up but some members, notably Mr. Spurley Hey, had been somewhat antagonistic to education by radio. However, Dr. Myers from the University of Manchester and Professor Moberly greatly encouraged the BBC and education authorities gradually funded sets in schools, and by the time Nichols moved south, 160 schools had wireless sets installed. With the formation of the Central Council for Schools' Broadcasting in 1928, all local lessons ceased, except in Scotland.

In order to cover a greater area of the North at reasonable cost, a low power 'relay' station was built in Sheffield and opened on 16 November, 1923. The idea was to be able to link Sheffield with Manchester by telephone line and transmit the Manchester programmes to the inhabitants of Sheffield. As well as having technical difficulties the scheme was not received well by the locals, who felt they should be entitled to their own station and their own programmes. In the end, a direct line to the London station satisfied the listeners, who obviously felt this gave them somewhat higher status.

From the first days of the move into Dickinson Street, the management realised that the quality of programmes would suffer because of the cramped and inhospitable conditions. A report on the station in 1924 stated: – 'The offices themselves are very cramped, dingy and suggestive of warehouse store rooms. The Station Director's room got so hot at times that it was impossible to stand it for more than ten minutes on end. The building is very slummy looking and callers have a choice of mounting something like 100 stairs or walking through a dirty alleyway into a cotton factory and then up in a goods hoist'. There was certainly a need for better premises and in December 1924, the studio and offices moved to the Orme Buildings in The Parsonage with the transmitter, now a 5kw RCA, remaining in Dickinson Street. Conducted tours were given of the new studios so the public could see the new opulent surroundings. There were two studios in the basement, one for orchestral and other music and a smaller one, more heavily damped, for talks and drama. Above the microphone in the talks studio hung the sign which gave 'Advice To Talkers'. These included, 'If you cough or rustle your papers you will deafen thousands'. It also stated 'Watch the red light. When it is alight the world can hear you.' It was a sign very familiar to John Beresford Clark who joined the station in 1924 and became official station announcer. The control was connected to the Dickinson Street transmitter by Post Office line. Most of the wiring was done by local staff who laboured round the clock for over a week to have the station ready for the opening.

More and more correspondence could be seen in the local press in praise or criticism of the station's output, one of the most discussed topics being the amount of time that the station used simultaneous broadcasts from London. There had been petitions when Basil Nichols had been Director, to try to reduce the output coming from London and now the new man in charge, Edward Liveing, had to answer the charges of too little local programming. He succeeded Nichols in September, 1925 and was the first official to be called North Regional Director.

SAVED BY TWO BOYS

Prompt Action Stops Fire in Big Building.

Orme Building, The Parsonage, Manchester, the home of 2ZY, the Manchester Broadcasting Station, and many other businesses, might have been seriously damaged by fire this morning had not a fifteen-years-old office boy's mother "dragged him out of bed" (to use his own expression) in good time for work.

The lad is George Griffiths, of 48, Orange-street, City Road, and he has only been working two days for the Electric Lamp Factors, Limited, in the first basement of Orme Building. Almost directly above are the offices of the First National Pictures, Limited, where there is a large stock of films in steel boxes.

Griffiths told a "Manchester Evening News" representative to-day how he saw the reflection of the fire through a glass window. He rushed upstairs and warned an older lad named William Moss, of Pringle Heath Road, Pendleton.

BROKE THE GLASS.

"I immediately sent Griffiths for a policeman," said Moss, "and, seizing a fire extinguisher, ran downstairs, broke the pane of glass in the door, and tried to put the fire out.

"Afterwards a fireman told me that to break a window or open a door was extremely dangerous, as the draught might have caused the flames to spread."

As it was, owing to the promptness of these two boys, there was little for the fire brigade to do.

The fire started in a wooden partition, in which was an electric fuse-box. Little damage was done.

Manchester Evening News, 26 October, 1926.

WIRELESS NOTES

VOICE AND PERSONALITY.

To-night occurs the first of the voice and personality tests, the details of which appeared in these notes on Wednesday last. The second will be on Thursday of this week, and the third on Friday.

During the tests nine different persons will read the same short story. The transmissions will be S.B. to all stations, and listeners will be asked to send in to the Manchester Station Director answers to the following questions in regard to each speaker:—

(1) Sex.
(2) Age.
(3) Profession or occupation, if any.
(4) Is the speaker accustomed to leading other people?
(5) Locality of his or her birth.
(6) Locality, if any, which has affected his or her speech.

Together with these answers listeners are also requested to give particulars as to the set they have used for listening (crystal or valve, headphone or loud-speaker), their own profession or occupation, and their address or locality. The information obtained will receive a careful preliminary sifting and classification at the Manchester Station, and will then be forwarded to Professor Pear, who will make a careful investigation of all the statistics available.

It is considered that this experiment will not only be of popular interest, but will also be of very considerable value to a branch of psychology which has not hitherto received a great deal of attention.

Manchester Guardian, 17 January, 1927.

Nº L 575707

RECEIVING LICENCE.

WIRELESS TELEGRAPHY ACT, 1904.

Mr. ....
(Name in full)

of .... is hereby
(Address in full)

authorised (subject in all respects to the conditions set forth on the back hereof) to establish a wireless station for the purpose of receiving messages at ....
(address of Station)

.... for a period ending on the last day of the month

of .... 192 . The payment of the fee of ten shillings is hereby acknowledged.
(date of expiration)

Dated ...... day of .... 192 .

Issued on behalf of the Postmaster-General

for Postmaster.

Signature of Licensee ....

If it is desired to continue to maintain the station after the date of expiration a fresh Licence must be taken out within fourteen days. Heavy penalties are prescribed by the Wireless Telegraphy Act, 1904, on conviction of the offence of establishing a wireless station without the Postmaster-General's Licence.

Stamp of Issuing Office.

The receiving licence was 10/-. As more and more people bought receivers so the press found news about the wireless from all quarters.

With still only a modest budget, the BBC in Manchester, as at other stations, was only too happy to put their microphones where there was to be an 'event' and obtain free broadcasts. Some outside broadcasts were, of course, paid for if the event was on a commercial basis, but in 1926 the BBC ran into a little trouble with its cathedral broadcasts. It was intended that every two months the station would broadcast a musical service from Manchester cathedral, but after the first of these one of the cathedral staff asked for contributions towards the 'Musical Services Fund'. The station had no money to allocate to what they envisaged as free broadcasting material and the programmes stopped for a time.

Public criticism of some of the station's output was countered by allowing certain members of the public to organise their own evening's entertainment. The Manchester Evening News was the first to be given this opportunity in November. Their choice of programme used the 2ZY Orchestra and Mr. Ralph Collis, 'a light comedian', to intersperse the musical items with 'Have you heard these?'. There was also the reading of an O. Henry story by James Bernard, 'one of the finest elocutionists'.

Such was the standing of broadcasting by 1926, that a civic reception was held in the Town Hall with many leading citizens present. Mr. J. C. W. Reith, the BBC's Managing Director, spoke on the influence of wireless on communal life and his speech, along with the evening's musical entertainment, was broadcast. The Dean of Manchester also spoke and commented that the 'wireless had been a great help in the improvement of public taste and the widening of public interest'.

The Manchester Station went through the General Strike without serious disruption to its output. BBC premises were protected by police and staff, but there proved to be little hostility to the BBC and the station developed as an enquiry bureau, as well as broadcasting proclamations, regulations and information. The importance of the medium to local listeners became obvious and stimulated an increase in the sale of wireless sets.

Chapter Four

REGIONAL FOCUS

The International Wireless Conference of 1926 decided on the need for substantial rearrangement of European broadcasting with a rationalisation of wavelengths and the need to reduce the number of stations. It was feared that Manchester was to lose its station, but the worry was illfounded and in 1927, the Manchester Evening Chronicle was able to report that Manchester was to serve the whole of the North and the transmitter was to be moved out of the city centre.

The Regional Scheme conceived by the BBC meant the building of several new transmitters throughout the country, the first one being Brookmans Park serving the London region. In the North a site was chosen at Moorside Edge, a spot near Huddersfield some 1100 feet above sea level. Three masts were planned, each of 500 feet and there was also the need to build a water storage tank for the station to hold 200,000 gallons, as water consumption would be as much as 10,000 gallons each day. The station also required a DC supply to be connected to the aerial wires outside normal broadcasting times to remove any ice formed, such was the bleak isolation of the site. The transmitter came into operation in May 1931, on 479m for regional transmissions, and a further transmitter for the National Programmes was opened in July, broadcasting on 301.5m. As Moorside Edge opened, so the relay transmitters at Liverpool, Stoke-on-Trent, Hull, Leeds, Sheffield and Bradford were closed. Some staff from these stations came to Manchester, notably Muriel Levy and Doris Gambell from 6LV, Liverpool.

The Liverpool station had opened in June 1924 on two floors above the Edinburgh Cafe, at the corner of the arcade and Lord Street. The first station director was H. C. Pearson (Uncle Pip) with Muriel Levy (Auntie Muriel) being only a part-time organiser. The Radio Circle had a membership of well over 5,000 by the time the transmitter closed in 1931. The station claimed to be the first regional station to broadcast the King's voice. With a station orchestra, military band and the regular use of the Liverpool Philharmonic Orchestra, the station had a reputation for quality musical broadcasts as well as the undoubted talents of Miss Levy in children's programmes.

H. C. Pearson (Uncle Pip) & Auntie Muriel Levy. *Two of the original broadcasters on the Liverpool Station.*

No. 33 Piccadilly. *Once known as the 'Temple of a Thousand Voices' the premises served the BBC for over forty-five years.*

The Leeds/Bradford Station (2LS) had opened on 8 July, 1924, in Cabinet Chambers, Basinghall Street. Cecil Bottle, the engineer, spent the opening night at the Bradford transmitter, which was near the railway station. The HT generator did not last long and he spent an hour sat astride it holding the brushes on with his hands. It was not long before the army complained that the transmitter interfered with training and it was moved to the other side of the city, away from the barracks.

In Sheffield, Fredrick Lloyd and his son Harry, had led the way with transmissions from their home in Ventnor Place, at their own expense. A transmitter (2UM) was established at the University under Lloyd's supervision. The Sheffield relay station had been the first in Yorkshire, launched on 16 November, 1923. It was known first as 6SL but changed to 6FL due to a clerical error at the Post Office. It took the Manchester programmes for six days and had its own on the seventh. Later it took all its programmes from London.

Station 6KH had opened in Hull on 16 August, 1924, in Bishops Lane. The receiver to pick up the Daventry signals was originally in the engineer's bedroom! Perhaps the most bizarre start to any station in the north was that of Newcastle (2NO), which had opened shortly after Manchester on 30 December, 1922, in Eldon Square. There had been a technical fault on that first night and the opening concert had to be given, for some reason, from the back of a lorry in a stable yard. Tom Payne was the first Director and his experience as a cinema manager and orchestra leader, enabled him to be announcer and play violin on the air. The Children's Hour had Sal Sturgeon who was 'Lizzie Ann, the Tyneside girl' and Auntie Julia.

Whilst at Orme Buildings, the British Broadcasting Company was transformed on 1 January, 1927, into a corporation under Royal Charter. The Regional Scheme, focusing Northern broadcasting on the Manchester station, gave new impetus to look for fresh premises yet again.

The Orme Buildings, although the best premises to date of the northern operation, were still not ideal and had many disadvantages. One often remembered was the close proximity to the River Irwell which, though allowing useful sound effects of water in some plays, required the staff to leave windows closed especially in hot weather because of the smell.

Eventually a building in Piccadilly was found and leased from the bank which occupied the ground floor frontage. It was estimated that the whole building was furnished for about £5,000, and in 1929, the dozen or so BBC staff moved across town. Now at No.33 Piccadilly there was more space with one large, two-storeys-high, gallery studio and three smaller ones, one having candles in a chandelier designed to induce just the right mood for 'talks'. A report was sent to London describing all the activities, in the hope that staffing levels would be increased. A subsequent visit to the station by the Director of Programmes concentrated on the facilities of the new premises and he noted, 'The general decorative effect looks a bit grim after Head Office, and the place needs freshening'. He also noted that there was noise from Piccadilly and recommended double glazing. Those first four studios were eventually added to and the Jacobean style decor updated in 1935 with art deco influence. The offices soon became too confining for the rapidly increasing numbers of staff and the upper floors of adjoining buildings were acquired.

During 1929, the committees which had been set up to advise on religious matters

The Manchester University Rag Magazine of 1928 contained some unusual wireless advertising.

were wound up and a Regional Religious Advisory Committee was established, meeting twice a year and under the chairmanship of the Bishop of Wakefield. Another development that same year was the studio time allowed various repertory bodies. Groups from Leeds, Liverpool, Sheffield and Hull were allowed to put on plays and the Manchester Studio Repertory Players was developed specialising in plays about the North and by Northern playwrights.

The practice of broadcasting variety performances from resorts such as Blackpool, Buxton, Morecambe and Grange-over-sands, which had begun some years earlier, was continued and microphones were taken to the Lake District and further afield. As well as these outside broadcasts there were 13 sports programmes, 41 concerts and 33 religious services in the 1929–30 period – a total of 298, of which 76 were taken nationally.

The first O.B. van was commissioned in 1926 to offset an excessive tax bill, and another was added in 1931 when the Outside Broadcast section was formed. Some landmarks in the service had been the first broadcast of a circus from Blackpool Tower, followed by a programme from Belle Vue Zoo in 1924 using a mobile transmitter in a pram; a show from the top of Blackpool Tower in 1928, and in the same year a mixup when the Prince of Wales was an hour late arriving to give a speech, again in Blackpool. By the time he arrived all but one engineer had left and he had to organise the whole broadcast himself!

One major technical achievement of 1930, was the broadcast of the maiden voyage of the MV Brittanic from the Liverpool pier head. A control point was set up on the landing stage with lines to the commentary box 150 yards away, to the pier head station to hear the whistle of the boat train, to the landing stage for effects of the luggage conveyor and on board the ship there were microphones in the engine room, purser's cabin, in the saloon to hear the orchestra and on the bridge. All the equipment and staff on board the boat went up the Clyde returning on another boat. It was technically 'very satisfying' and a big hit with listeners.

The co-ordination of eight transmitters in the Regional Scheme led to a considerable increase in the quality of the O.B.'s with the establishment of a 'flying squad' of engineers, and a speech given by the Prince of Wales in the Free Trade Hall, Manchester was 'miked up' with one hour's notice. By 1933, the section boasted two drivers and eleven engineers.

As well as an expansion of the outside broadcasts in the 1930s, so in other departments significant staff changes were taking place. With only a week to see how Derek McCulloch (Uncle Mac) was running the London Children's Hour, Olive Shapley started work in 1934 as North Regional Children's Hour Organiser, calling herself 'Anna'. On leaving Oxford, Miss Shapley had hoped to become a teacher and did give some WEA lectures for a time. With no full-time job on the horizon, she took up a nursery-school training course in London. Prospects were looking a little bleak when her mother saw an advertisement for the 'Organiser of Northern Children's Hour'. Her first remark was, 'But I hate the wireless!'. She applied and got the job, and now says she 'never ceased to bless that day'. Still broadcasting today, she has become one of the most respected figures in Northern broadcasting.

Thrown in at the deep end in 1934, she was lucky to find several experienced professionals to help her. There was Doris Gambell and Muriel Levy who, as well

Olive Shapley. *One of the most loved and respected broadcasters in the North of England. Her varied contributions to the art of broadcasting have spanned well over fifty years and continue today.*

as singing and acting, wrote two or three sketches each week for the 'Hour'. Other regulars were Harry Hopewell, Noel Morris and pianist Charles Kelly. These were soon joined by Violet Carson who started work for the BBC in 1935.

Miss Carson had played for silent films and learnt much of her craft accompanying 'artists' on the popular concerts at the Ambassador in Pendleton, Salford. She often used to say, 'After the Ambassador you can do anything!'. One of her two referees for the job was the famous comedian Norman Evans whom she had met in her cinema days. She wrote later of her audition, 'I was petrified. I sat in Piccadilly Gardens for half an hour, working up enough courage to go into the BBC building. I had a cup of tea in the Kardomah cafe and nearly decided to go home, instead'. Luckily she didn't and that Kardomah cafe became a regular stop each day before her performances. She was offered a 15 minute spot for £2.10s. which she did and was paid in cash on the spot. David Porter, the programme announcer, recommended Miss Carson to some of the influential heirarchy and she was offered a concert where she first met Muriel Levy and Doris Gambell. She was personally thanked by the show's producer, John Salt, who was impressed by her obvious talents. Messrs. Levy, Gambell and Carson later formed an informal singing group known as The Three Semis, and Auntie Vi's radio career never looked back.

One evening years later, when the recording link to London was broken, Miss Carson entertained the cast of nervous children to a song about the occupants of a Manchester Street, where each character was described to her young audience. One member of that audience was a fourteen-year-old boy called Tony Simpson, who later changed his name to Tony Warren and years later devised a television drama which he once said may well have been stimulated by that song. He showed the first script to Olive Shapley who, as she is regularly reminded, told him it was a little boring and the idea was later formerly turned down by the BBC. The television series was Coronation Street and gave rise to Violet Carson's third career just when she was thinking of permanent retirement.

Under Miss Shapley's direction and that of Nan Macdonald who took over in 1938, the Children's programmes went from strength to strength. Children were encouraged to present their own programmes, whether variety or the 'Your Own Ideas' programmes and literally thousands of auditions were held. Nursery Sing Songs began in 1938 and went on for over twenty years. There was much fine drama and varieties like the 'Stuff And Nonsense' shows. Eric Fogg endeared himself to children with his earwig in a matchbox, and Grizzle the dragon, and often added after the goodbyes '. . . and spookler from Uncle Eric'. But perhaps best remembered and loved were the Romany programmes.

The Reverend Bramwell Evens had begun his weekly rambles two years before Miss Shapley arrived in Manchester, and by 1934 they were the most popular programmes on that station. Evens, ordained in 1908, was an experienced public speaker, and travelling as he did about the countryside, had taught himself the ways of the open air. He was descended from the famous gypsy Cornelius Smith and had bought himself a caravan, or vardo as it is called in Romany, in 1921. He had given talks to schools in Manchester and when his name was mentioned to Olive Schill, then the Manchester Organiser, she offered him an audition and a programme the next month. He did not want to be called Uncle Bramwell or the Reverend Bramwell

41

Romany – Reverend Bramwell Evens. *'He loved birds and green places and the wind on the heath, and saw the brightness of the skirts of God.' – (Inscription on a cot in Birkenhead Hospital dedicated to the memory of Romany.)*

Evens and on the spur of the moment he suggested 'the Romany'. It was on 7 October, 1932, that the Radio Times announced, 'We meet the Romany, and learn all about the gypsy trail'. Other favourites like the Kookaburra and Rosemary stories alternated with his talks. The first programme was 'impromptu fun' with two short stories told by Evens but soon the formula of Romany taking his two questioning friends, Muriel (Levy) and Doris (Gambell), for nature rambles, became established. The questions and answers were often unscripted and the spontaneity, along with the excellent sound effects, created an atmosphere like no other programme before had done.

Jack Hollinshead was the one who supplied those evocative sound effects, either by using records or mechanically reproducing the sounds of the open air in the studio. He had joined the BBC in 1930 at the early age of 14 as effects assistant, and moved up to become in charge of the department called upon by numerous producers to set the scene for the listener. At first all he had to play with was a set of three records, each with twelve tracks. All other effects were produced on the spot like lead shot rocking to and fro in a cardboard box to give the impression of seawash, or using a wire whisk on a tin box to achieve the sound of a train. On one memorable occasion, he was asked by Victor Smythe to provide effects for a world war one drama called 'Red Night'. The attic of broadcasting house was set up as trenches, and fireworks were electrically detonated to provide the explosions. The effects were so realistic, that the room had to be replastered afterwards. The Romany country walks were believed by many to actually be in the open and when the Radio Times published an article telling listeners how it was all done, a silly storm blew up with listeners writing in to complain that they had been deceived. Nothing was further from the station's intention, but for some, that explanation caused the magic to be lost.

The Romany programmes were broadcast nationally from the North for many years, but Derek McCulloch took a lot of persuading at first. He too was a great nature lover and perhaps he thought this was a challenge to his domain. For Nan Macdonald, producer of the Romany programmes as Children's Hour organiser, this was just one of the many battles she had with 'head office' in London. Her determination was more often than not rewarded and in the case of Romany, Mac eventually agreed and Evens gained tens of thousands more fans.

It was Evens' intimate knowledge and obvious love of the countryside which held children and adults spellbound as he made his weekly excursions. In one of his broadcasts he said, 'When you get fed up with present-day happenings, go out into the lanes and the fields, and listen and look at the things of Nature. There is no hurry in that world – that is why I am a dodderer. I lose all sense of time when I'm in the country, forget the speed of machinery . . . To be a dodderer is a lost art these days, and one that we should recapture.'

On 20 November, 1943, after digging in his garden, Romany died and the whole country was shocked. Some school classes had to be cancelled the following day as children proved unconsolable. Condolences and appreciations flooded in to the BBC and many children wrote in asking about the fate of Raq, Romany's dog, who followed him on his numerous 'rambles'. For millions of adults too, Tuesday nights would not be the same. Romany's caravan was parked near his home in Wilmslow, almost as a memorial to the much-loved personality, and was opened to the public on 2 October, 1944, in a spot where it still stands today. This touching appreciation was written by

Geoffrey Dearmer, the London Children's Hour producer.

'Goodbye, dear friend. If no more we shall roam
Fresh woods with you, nor fields your voice made cool;
Nor find the fieldmouse in his harvest home,
The brown trout in his pool.

Nor with hands made more gentle with your words,
Pick up the shrew mouse or the trembling hare;
Nor, with ears wiser, name the singing birds
In trees no longer bare.

If we no more with you shall do these things,
Let us, at least, say sometimes when the clear
Spring skies are full of song and woods with wings,
'I wish that he was here.'

Then shall we keep your memory green and true;
Then shall the lovely world more lovely grow,
And you, dear Romany, I think of you
Would wish to have it so.'

On the anniversary of his death, a memorial service was broadcast, the above appreciation was read and one of the very few recordings of his programmes was repeated.

One of the most famous names in Northern broadcasting, he began his career in the early 1930's. He drove from his home in Southport in his Austin Seven, no doubt rehearsing the lines of his audition readings, and arrived in Piccadilly a little before his 4 pm appointment. He sat with several others in the waiting room before being ushered into the studio to give his readings from Hamlet, St. John Irving's 'The Ship', Hindle Wakes and some lines from Sean O'Casey's plays. It was ten days later that a letter arrived from Jan Bussell, then head of the North Region drama department. Wilfred Pickles' name was to be added to the Department's list of players. His first play was with the excellent North Country actor Frank Nichols, whose place as premier actor on the station, Pickles was eventually to fill, as Nichols' health faded. Bussell, who gave much encouragement to Pickles, went on to form the famous puppet theatre with Ann Hogarth.

Pickles was given more and more work, especially on the Children's Hour, and moved to Manchester. He also worked in productions by Geoffrey Bridson, and a newcomer to the Northern studios, Cecil McGivern, though nothing was allowed to interfere with Pickles' work on Children's Hour. Other departments offered more prestigious parts and better contracts, but Pickles was devoted to, or perhaps too frightened to disobey, the Hour's producer Nan Macdonald. Trevor Hill remembered that 'Miss Dora Broome of No. 2, Railway Sidings, Douglas, Isle of Man, could never get over the fact that THE Wilfred Pickles read her Matilda Mouse stories, not just for the North but throughout the whole British Isles'. His versatility as an actor is remembered by Olive Shapley who was amazed at the ease with which, during a production on the French Revolution, he could switch from being an aristocrat dying on the guillotine to being the leader of the hostile crowd, dozens of times.

The Three Semis. *Messrs. Levy, Gambell and Carson. All individually talented the three came together as a trio regularly in Northern Children's Hour. This photograph was taken in October 1951.*

'Have A Go.' *Pickles this time at Cresswell Colliery Miners' Institute. On stage are Joe Browne (accordianist), Philip Robinson (next to miner), Pickles and P. Dobson with the gong. Miss Irwin sits with the 'quiz money'.*

Out of the blue, Pickles was given the holiday relief announcer's job by John Salt, the region's Programme Director, joining Freddy Allen and Humphrey Donner. As well as announcing he also took part in plays, such as 'Billy Welcome', and introduced 'Kingpins of Comedy'. During the war he moved to London and became famous as the announcer with the northern accent, and his famous 'Good neet' angered as many as it pleased. On his return to the North he took on numerous roles until John Salt again changed his life. Salt had recently visited America and had returned with the idea of an audience participation game inspired by the quiz shows he had heard on American stations. He suggested that Pickles was just the man to host the show. The first idea for a title was 'Quiz Bang' but Pickles said he would never appear in a show called 'Quiz Bang'. The next suggestion was 'Have a Go, Joe'. Jack Jordan went off and soon came back with the signature tune: –

Have a go, Joe. Come on and have a go.
You can't lose ow't, it costs you nowt
To make yourself some dough.
So hurry up and join us,
Don't be shy and don't be slow.
Come on, Joe! Have a Go!

The show was originally produced by Philip Robinson in Leeds with Jack Jordan's Orchestra, but when Robinson moved to Manchester to take over outside broadcasts from Victor Smythe, Barney Colehan joined the programme. The orchestra was dropped in favour of pianist Violet Carson and with 'Mabel at the table' the show became an institution. Phrases like 'She's a bobby dazzler', 'Are yer courtin?' and 'Give him the money, Barney!' echoed throughout the country, the latter phrase referring to Colehan giving out the prizes. Pickles presented 'the people to the people' with the programme developing into numerous chats with contestants, as Colehan saw this was Pickles' great talent, and the quiz itself became almost incidental. The programme was finally shelved in January, 1967. With no cast, props, script or rehearsals, the show was a unique achievement and a personal triumph for Pickles.

It was in 1937 that Godfrey Talbot joined the ranks of the staff of the North Region as Press Officer. Talbot had spent several years in Manchester working on the ill-fated City News, and after its closure, the Daily Dispatch, and had found Manchester in the early thirties 'rare and inspiring'. From his new small office overlooking Piccadilly, Talbot set to work to publicise the talents that were around him: the young Tyneside ex-schoolteacher Cecil McGivern's strong regional plays; Donald Boyd, from the Guardian, making the Talks Department distinguished; productions of talented poet John Pudney; the stylish Hubert Foster Clark as Director of Music was continuing the station's tradition of musical excellence, and D. G. Bridson promoting the North in new and revolutionary documentary forms. Talbot especially praised the talents of Archie Harding who came from London to become North Region Programme Director. His forthright approach and left wing views had caused Reith to move him north where, he said, 'you can't do much damage'.

'It was Harding', Talbot wrote, 'who was one of the first people to see the quality of an unkempt girl named Joan Littlewood, who in his Manchester days had tramped up from London to knock on the BBC's Northern drama door.' The north itself was not short of talent with such names as Robert Donat, Peter Glenville and Wendy Hiller beginning their acting careers in the 'old tram-shed' that was the Rusholme Repertory Theatre.

The Regional Scheme was, of course, administered from London and an example of the interplay between co-ordinators in London and the Regional Directors is quoted by Asa Briggs, when Harding in Manchester insisted to Lindsay Wellington in London that a Sunday concert given by Pablo Casals should not be broadcast by his region. Instead he wanted to broadcast a concert by a Merseyside Orchestra of unemployed musicians. Wellington argued that the Casals concert was too important to drop, but Harding insisted that the programme of the unemployed musicians was 'of great social importance' and did not want to disappoint them. Harding won the day, but an understanding between the two caused problems like that not to occur again.

Harding was an Oxford graduate and had begun his career on radio, producing plays in London before being put in charge of feature programmes in Manchester. Bridson, who started in radio under Harding's wing, said that Harding believed that all people should be encouraged to express their views and that their views should be heard, no matter what their social class. These opinions gave rise to the type of dramatised journalism which Bridson and others on the station developed. Recording equipment was initially very un-portable. The station had a Blattnerphone using steel tape on which to record, and more recently acquired acetate disc cutters which allowed some freedom to record outside the studio.

It was thought too dangerous to have unscripted speeches and many people interviewed had to put their thoughts in writing in order to read them later in the studio. The results were very forced, stunted and unemotional. Bridson and other producers like Francis Dillon eventually got better results by recording people in their own homes, even though their interviews were still scripted. Bridson's first feature play, using voice recordings linked with a story theme, was 'The March of the '45' which was broadcast in 1936. Other drama documentaries followed, many having live orchestras playing specially commissioned music. William Walton and Benjamin Britten's first radio commissioned music was part of Douglas Bridson's 'King Arthur' in 1937. To facilitate the use of numerous recordings, Bridson used the device of a central character to act as interlocutor. The character of Harry Hopeful was invented and played by a clock repairer and amateur actor from Irlam called Frank Nichols. Hopeful went round the region looking for work and interviewed locals as he went. Bridson was also to create 'Billy Welcome' and 'Ex-Corporal Wilf' for Wilfred Pickles. In a report to London in 1935, Liveing stated that he felt Brisdon, recently made Head of Drama, 'though not an impressive man to meet, could deliver the goods'. This proved to be totally correct.

Others in the group that Harding gathered around him were Kenneth Adam, who later went on to become Director of Television, Ewan MacColl, the singer, whom Adam first saw busking outside the Manchester Paramount cinema in 1933, Edgar Lustgarten, Jan Bussell and Joan Littlewood who married MacColl, and the nucleus of her Theatre Workshop was formed from the group of radio actors from Manchester. The Manchester radio drama 'school' of the thirties, as well as being innovative, gave voice to a regional expression little heard before nationally. The radical approach

The March of the '45

A Radio Panorama
in Verse and Song

by

D. G. BRIDSON

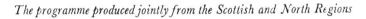

in which the march of
Prince Charles Edward is
followed from the landing at Loch Nan Uamh to the final
defeat at Culloden Moor

The programme produced jointly from the Scottish and North Regions

PART I
'The High Endeavour'
Produced by Gordon Gildard (*From Scottish*)

PART II
'The Turn of the Tide'
Produced by D. G. Bridson (*From North*)

PART III
'Time's Last Syllable'
(*From North and Scottish*)

Musical arrangements by David Stephen and Crawford McNair

TONIGHT AT 9.40

The March of the '45. *D. G. Bridson's classic anthology broadcast on 10 November, 1936.*

Saturday
NORTH
668 kc/s, 449.1 m.

DORIS GAMBELL
sings with Jack Hardy's Little Orchestra in 'Dance and Duet', this evening at 7.50.

10.15 THE DAILY SERVICE

Time Signal, Greenwich, at 10.30

10.30 Weather Forecast for Farmers and Shipping

10.45-5.0 Regional Programme

5.0 THE CHILDREN'S HOUR
(*See page 87*)

6.0 Regional Programme

6.30 FURTHER FAMILIAR FABLES
No. 7—' Jungle High Jinks! '
Another of Æsop's Fables told in a new way with words and music by Henry Reed
The music played by a section of The BBC Northern Orchestra
Led by Harold Jones
Conducted by H. Foster Clark
Produced by David Porter
This evening you will meet all the animals of earlier Fables broadcasts —including the Lion, the Wolf, the Fox, Mrs. Crow, and the Three Little Frogs—in an animal jamboree, culminating in a race between the Hare and the Tortoise.

7.0 SPOTLIGHT ON SPORT
Newcastle United
v.
Sheffield United
An eye-witness account

7.4 A conversation on Rugby Union
arranged by H. A. Clayton-Greene

7.16 app. Arsenal
v.
Huddersfield Town
An eye-witness account

7.20 Northern Sports Bulletin

7.30 'FLORA'S HOLIDAY'
A cycle of old English melodies by H. Lane Wilson
The Northumbrian Quartet:
Ada Alsop (soprano) ; Margaret Magnay (mezzo-soprano) ; James Etherington (tenor) ; Fred McIntyre (baritone)
Quartet : Come all ye lads and lasses
Soprano : Love's Greeting
Tenor : Tell me charming creatures
Quartet : Gentle Dawn
Quartet : The Country Dance
Mezzo-soprano : Maidens, beware ye!
Baritone : Sound Argument
A Catch, The Pedlar
Quartet : The Commotion of Love
(*Stagshaw*)

7.50 'DANCE AND DUET'
The Little Orchestra directed by Jack Hardy
with
Doris Gambell (soprano)
and
W. B. MacMillan (tenor)

8.30 'THE SHEPHERDS'
A radio version of The Wakefield Second Shepherds' Play
modernised and arranged by James R. Gregson
Cast
First Shepherd........Frank Crosland
Second Shepherd....James R. Gregson
Third Shepherd.........Joe Illingworth
Mak.................................F. A. Bean
Gill.........................Florence Gregson
Angel.......................Mildred Dyson
Mary.......................Jessica Dunning
Produced by Edward Wilkinson
This is hardly a Nativity play at all, though it has a tailpiece of religious significance. It is an early character-comedy of English literature, full of lively Northern humour.

9.0 Regional Programme

10.0 *Time Signal, Greenwich*
THE FOURTH NEWS
(including Weather Forecast)
NEWS TALKS and SPORT

10.30 JACK HYLTON AND HIS BAND
with
June Malo
Peggy Dell
Doreen Stevens
Maureen Potter
(*Regional*)

Time Signal, Greenwich, at 11.30

11.50-12.0 **NEWS SUMMARY**
including Weather Forecast

December 1938. *A typical Saturday evening's entertainment from the North Region.*

gave rise to many clashes with Lawrence Gilliam in London who, although he disapproved of much that Harding was doing, was courageous enough to allow it.

Kenneth Adam, along with Donald Boyd, Robert Kemp and E. R. Thompson were perloined from the Manchester Guardian by Harding, who built up a highly professional and loyal team. He was always pleased to affirm that 'Anything London can do, we can do better'.

Until Philip Robinson took over from him, Victor Smythe continued to produce numerous variety shows from a multitude of venues. One of the most ambitious was for the August Bank Holiday in 1937, when he organised seventeen different locations for engineers around Blackpool. Microphones were in the Pleasure Beach, Stanley Park, at the Tower Circus and many presented live acts from the galaxy of stars that were performing at the resort. George Formby, Tessie O'Shea, Harry Korris, Reginald Dixon and many more featured, along with several dance bands, in the 75 minute show.

When Liveing left the station in 1937, he broadcast a farewell in which he observed that the BBC's policy of regional areas had 'marked out more definitely than ever before the somewhat vague entities of the English Provinces themselves'.

By the late thirties, with the expectation of war, much of the time in Piccadilly was spent in precautions and preparations for the inevitable conflict to come. Programmes suffered as staff had to attend lectures and drills, and by 1938 staff dispersal plans were complete.

Radio Times Illustration

Chapter Five

THE FORTIES

By the time war was announced on 3 September, 1939, John Coatman had been North Regional Director for 18 months. Coatman was to encourage many new ideas and promote regional programmes. Described by Pickles as looking more like a farmer than Regional Director, (perhaps second only to Freddy Allen as the untidiest dresser in the Manchester studios), his appearance belied a shrewd and discerning mind, and a friendly and fatherly personality. It was Coatman who guided the region through the turmoil of the war.

Manchester, like the other regions, had been told two days before the declaration of war to open its 'war stations' sealed orders and within half an hour, at 8.15 pm, the Home Service was heard for the first time.

At 4 o'clock on the afternoon of 3 September, Manchester was told by London that the Children's Hour was to be cancelled. The afternoon's rehearsals were wasted and the staff sent home. The Manchester station was silenced – regional broadcasting had ceased. Pickles and Allen were kept on as announcers with no programmes to announce and they spent much of their time covering the windows with black paint.

In London many departments were already on their way out to Bristol, and Sandy Macpherson was filling in with numerous organ programmes. Soon the various departments settled in their new homes, the London administration was reorganised and Manchester was given some air time. The Northern Orchestra and Children's Hour were two of the first items to be broadcast.

The Commissionaires suddenly regained a lost authority. The ex-servicemen had sufficient experience to train the staff as members of the Home Guard. Thus one, Pat McGlyn, was able to order about senior officials in the makeshift parade ground of one studio. Staff took their duties seriously. Certain senior staff were trained by the police as incident officers, being able to take charge in case of emergency. This had been requested by the BBC and several members of staff had lessons in fire extinguishing, mustard gas decontamination, first aid and the organisation of emergency services. As a test, a volunteer was required to be tested in a mock emergency. Basil Vernon, then Chief Engineer, stepped forward and an incident was

John Coatman. *Director/Controller, North Region 1938–1949.*

enacted. Vernon made a control room in the basement and set to work to unravel the difficulties the police dreamed up – a mustard gas casualty on the roof to be brought down by extending ladder, a bomb in one of the studios, fires throughout the building with ambulance, fire, police and demolition services being called – and all in two hours! Vernon remembered that when the onslaught was over, he was unable to sleep that night, and after relating his evening's exploits to the rest of the staff, there were no more volunteers. Luckily there were no such actual incidents for the whole of the hostilities.

The BBC Drama Department was originally sent from London to Evesham, but Val Gielgud protested at the inadequate space and facilities, and on 16 November, 1939, the department set up home in Manchester. This move cut the producers off from their contacts with the London theatre and caused them to mix with the group of features' producers under Harding. The severely restricted supply of experienced actors caused the station to re-form the Drama Repertory Company with regularly employed personnel. The original Repertory Company had been disbanded in 1931, as it was thought that the public was tired of hearing the same old voices. However, the company formed in 1939, is still in existence. Gladys Young, Philip Wade, Laidman Browne, Ivan Sampson, Valentine Dyall and many other fine actors moved north. Regular staff began to take in their stride the comings and goings of such famous stars as John Clements and Laurence Olivier, who, still in his Fleet Air Arm uniform, just popped in to do a play. Thus a small group of actors, actresses, engineers and producers became very experienced in radio technique, and the talent of Gielgud brought a new excellence to radio drama. In 1941, the Features and Drama departments moved back to London.

There was continual criticism from Manchester that the regional contributions to national broadcasting were insufficient. In 1943, the northern Ministry of Information Committee demanded full restoration of regional broadcasting as soon as possible. Roger Eckersley, then Assistant Controller (Regions), visited the Manchester station at about this time and remarked on the 'old-fashioned and rather too small' premises at Piccadilly, which, although they offered a pleasant view of 'the square', needed to be double glazed because of the endless procession of trams.

About 2,500 outside broadcasts emanated from the region during the war, presenting engineers and commentators with endless difficulties. In the bad winters of 1939, '40 and '41 cables often had to be dug out from under snow by bands of engineers camped out on bleak moors, and commentators often worked 24 hours to make recordings in foul conditions. The Outside Broadcast Department was using an enormous Thornycroft Pantechnicon as a mobile recording and broadcasting unit. Recordings were made on acetate disc cutters, powered by batteries, which were charged up as the vehicle travelled all over the North of England and Scotland. Trevor Hill recalled that certain hump-back bridges were noted as 'impassable for recording purposes'.

Coatman in 1944 again complained at the lack of air time for specifically northern programmes. He mentioned the number of servicemen overseas who were from the North and who would, of course, appreciate sounds from their home. The output of the northern studios had increased from the average pre-war monthly output of 75

Fred Fairclough (looking remarkably like Wilfred Pickles) introducing 'Strike A Home Note'. *This edition in April 1944 came from Coln Municipal Hall. The series came from a different area each week and transmitted on the General Forces network especially for the soldiers abroad who came from that week's location.*

Weekly Press Meeting in the Board Room of Broadcasting House, and overseen by B.W. Cave-Browne-Cave and Reginald Jordan, extreme left.

hours to well over 100 hours. In 1942, for example, engineers organised 476 outside broadcasts which included major projects such as the enthronement of the Archbishop of York and the Trades Union Congress in Blackpool. Major events like these were transmitted worldwide, as were more homely pictures of the north in programmes like 'Back Home' and 'This England'. Workers' Playtime visited over 400 factories by the end of the war, many of which were organised by the Outside Broadcast Department in Manchester.

As battles raged throughout Europe, D. G. Bridson produced 'We Speak for Ourselves' and 'Transatlantic call' and McGivern gave us 'Battle of Britain' and 'Fighter Pilot'. As the troups moved through Alamein, programmes like 'Home Flash' and 'Strike A Home Note' were broadcast featuring schools' choirs, colliery bands and northern folk songs, bringing soldiers sound pictures of their home towns.

Music continued to play a large part in the broadcasting timetable, not only on record and in concerts, but also as specially written and arranged material in features, and incidental music in plays. The talents of Henry Reed were often used in such arrangements. Reed had played with the Henry Hall band at the Midland Hotel and Gleneagles. After Hall joined the BBC, Reed left and approached Archie Harding for a job as arranger, writer and conductor. Eventually he had his own programmes like 'The Music Shop' playing original compositions and 'Everybody Swing'. It was he who arranged Messrs. Carson, Gambell and Levy into the 'Three Semis', and by the late thirties was regularly contributing to Children's Hour. It was noticed that he always contrived to cause the end of his orchestra rehearsals to coincide with the public bar opening times.

Richard North became Head of Variety and had the idea of a series of fifteen minute interviews with famous comedians. The series was called 'Kingpins of Comedy' and Wilfred Pickles was the interviewer. North also gave Pickles the chance to join forces with Jack Train in 'Two's a Crowd' which consisted of a series of sketches where the two entertainers could display their talents at numerous accents and mimicry. The show was broadcast on the Forces Programme. The 'Harry Hopeful' series was revived and the 'Billy Welcome' propaganda programmes again featured Pickles.

Ralph Truman joined the staff in Manchester when Freddy Allen left for London. Robert Robinson joined him before Pickles also moved south. The Children's Hours maintained their high standard throughout the war, though at the beginning there had been numerous letters from Nan MacDonald to Derek McCullock protesting at the lack of national air time for the Manchester 'Hour'. Romany became a national celebrity during the war until his sad death in 1943.

Months before the ending of hostilities, the Director General, Sir William Haley, promised that within ninety days of the end of the war, the Regional Service would return. On 23 July, 1945, the 'Home' and 'Light' programmes began drawing on the regional contributions. The North Region revelled in its new freedom with an increase in outside broadcasts and an influx of new producers.

It was in 1945 that the North acquired its first News Editor in the shape of Robert Reid, who joined the station after his duty as BBC war correspondent. On 2ZY, news had been mainly in the form of service announcements under the supervision of the

Station Director. From 1923 regular bulletins had been broadcast from Manchester and Newcastle, twice each week night and once on Sunday. These were relayed from London and followed by brief local news. There had also been specialist bulletins on subjects such as farming and scouting.

After the instigation of the Regional Scheme, the Northern News came into being, restricted to Saturday evenings. A late night news was later established, with much of the 'copy' coming from the Manchester Evening News, to whom a payment was made for distribution amongst the reporters. There was a 'gentleman's agreement' that broadcast news would not go out while evening papers were still on the streets. Payment to the M.E.N. was not very satisfactory and there grew up a feeling with reporters that 'any old thing would do for the BBC'. Even direct payment to journalists proved unsatisfactory. Compilation of items was then the responsibility of the Talks Department. Press officers became involved with the ever growing workload, including Reid when he was in that position. When he returned as News Editor, Reid built up a network of accredited reporters. With the help and experience of Coatman, the assistance of Vernon Noble and the free reign given to them by John Salt, the service expanded to two nightly bulletins, a news magazine, 'Northern Newsreel', a weekly farming programme, and a Saturday night sports programme, and the small group also compiled news items for the national news.

Reid went to Hamburg and approached several members of the British Forces Network, offering positions in the North. Ray Lakeland, Trevor Hill, Alan Clarke and Barney Colehan were some who made their name in the North from this source. Over the next few years a tremendous effort was made to revitalise news coverage with newcomers Lakeland, Kenneth Wolstenholme, Kevin McGarry and later David Coleman and Alan Dixon.

Noble temporarily succeeded Reid until James Bell took over, and again the news coverage increased with additional Friday night Northern Newsreel and sports programmes, the occasional news feature and increased contributions to national news. The region began sending film contributions to television news, using at first, freelance and agency cameramen. In 1957, the region began its own television news programmes.

In 1946, the Variety Department held two thousand auditions to identify new talent in the area. Those successful were given their first chance on the air in such programmes as 'Curtains Up' and 'Stay at Home', and the best of them were heard again on 'R.S.V.P.'. The Northern Orchestra gave seventy public performances in 1946 and, on the invitation of the Manchester Corporation, began Wednesday midday promenade concerts. From the North East there was 'Wot Cheor Geordie', and other light entertainment programmes. In that same year 'Public Enquiry' began a long series of live discussions on controversial subjects.

Drama had been minimal in the region after the Drama Department returned to London, but by the end of the 1940's full production was restored, not least because of the establishing of an experimental school for radio dramatists in Leeds. The use of tape recording techniques gave outside broadcasts more scope and before the end of the 1940's, the enthusiasm and talent in the area led the North Region Director to write, 'The broadcasting potentialities of the North of England are on a national scale, and their exploitation is limited only by the restrictions of staff and gear and time'.

Chapter Six
POST WAR RADIO

In August 1950, D. Stephenson, who had taken over from Coatman in 1949 as Controller, North Region, wrote a highly critical review of the station, its programmes, its staff and its future. Since the war the station had found its feet again but the illness and death of John Salt, then Head of Programmes, had caused great problems. Salt had heroically tried to resist the effects of his illness but inevitably there had been a 'loosening of programme control'. Salt had been held in great esteem by his staff, always open to new ideas and, as Herbert Smith recalled 'If the item was a success it was your success. If it failed it was his failure. He was a big man physically and mentally'

Bryan W. Cave–Brown–Cave was appointed Acting Head of North Regional Programmes until Robert Stead took on the role without a great deal of previous experience. He and Stephenson were somewhat critical of the standard of the producers in the region, and even though six new producers were sent from London, they would have preferred quality to quantity. Drama, Talks and News departments were reasonably satisfactory and the Features department, although several good staff had left, young men like J. Bridges, T. Hill and an unknown quantity Denis Mitchell, showed potential. Stephenson remarked that the Department 'should find itself after a few rough passages. If it doesn't, we shall get the press-gang at work again.' Other areas *e.g.* Children's, Religious and Music received limited praise, but the Variety Department and Outside Broadcasts received the severest criticism and these were drastically reorganised.

It was Robert Stead who, as a producer in 1947, had hit on the idea of a gardener's forum. Enthusiastic about outside broadcasts he booked a room in the Broad Oak Hotel, Ashton-under-Lyne and invited the Smallshaw Gardening Society to provide the audience. The programme was originally entitled 'How Does Your Garden Grow' and subtitled 'Gardeners' Question Time', but it soon became known by the subtitle and has run from that day to this. Two of the original team were Fred Loads and Bill Sowerbutts and Dr. (later Professor) Alan Gemmell joined what was to become a regular core of experts on the programme in 1950, with Stead as question master.

Robert Stead. *Producer and later Controller, North Region.*

Gardener's Question Time. *Left to Right. Fred Loads, Franklyn Engelmann, Alan Gemmell and Bill Sowerbutts.*

Joan Littlewood and Nan Macdonald talk to the people of Edale for a Children's Hour feature on Derbyshire.

Freddy Grisewood became the chairman of the programme, to be followed by Franklin Engelmann. On the eve of the 1000th programme, Englemann died. 'Jingles' last words were reportedly 'What is Ken going to do tomorrow?'. 'Ken' was Ken Ford, who, by then, had become the regular producer. It was he who had to chair the special edition in the Royal Horticultural Society's Hall in Westminster, which was naturally overshadowed by Engelmann's death. A happier anniversary was marked by the planting of 'Fred Loads' in Mr. Middleton's memorial garden near Cavendish Square in London. This particular Fred Loads was a variety of rose specially named by Fryers of Knutsford, after the veteran broadcaster.

The Children's Hour in Manchester was innovative in the regular use of local child actors and actresses. After the war there was a definite policy to make plays more realistic and less 'pony riding, who's for tennis'. They wanted to use real children with local accents. Many of them came to broadcasting via local acting and dance schools. Brian Trueman, who luckily had not lost his Manchester accent at drama school, started on the station in 1946 in a programme called Plover Patrol and was an old hand by the time Billie Whitelaw, Judith Chalmers, Peter Wheeler and others came. Beryl Bainbridge wrote as a child for the Northern Children's Hour at the start of her writing career. Herbert Smith taught the young actors and actresses microphone technique, and with encouragement from other experienced actors like Violet Carson and Wilfred Pickles, the group could turn their hand, not only to plays on Children's Hour, but Saturday Night Theatre or situation comedy programmes. Plays were either staged in the large drama studio number one, or in two small studios, numbers three and five, up on the top floor. One was for indoor acoustics and one for outdoor, specially deadened for no echo. This, of course, meant that actors were constantly running from one room to the other while either a linking piece of music played or one actor spoke to cover the others' movement.

The station attempted one of the first soap operas called 'Seven O'clock at the Willows' later shortened to 'At The Willows', which predated 'The Archers' and was a most ambitious project. The producer was Alick Hayes, who later produced the 'Just William' programmes, and there was a resident five piece orchestra to play incidental music, composed for each episode, as well as the signature tune. Hayes was disorganised and proper rehearsals were almost non-existent. Trueman recalls one episode where his script was rewritten as he was reading it!

In 1951, the Fifty-One Society was formed at the request of the North Region. Named after the year of its foundation and the number of its members, it was independent of the BBC, but its proceedings, which consisted of speeches, discussion and debate were broadcast. Lord Beveridge was the opening guest speaker, and over the years the programme discussed a wide range of topics from advertising to the hydrogen bomb, religious topics and the welfare state, and was innovative in this type of programming. By 1952 it was reported that the Talks Department had improved its quality and regular output now offered 'Tuesday Talk', 'Question Time' and 'Progress Report' as well as 'The Fifty-One Society', and the ever faithful 'Gardeners' Question Time'. Though the quality had certainly improved, listening figures appeared to have diminished. All departments had shown improvement, including sports commentaries, even though difficulties with the commentary of the Grand National had caused questions in Parliament!

In the fifties, excellent drama and features programmes were produced, including 'The Drifting Sort' (about tramps), 'Pity My Simplicity' (mentally defective children), 'For Valour' (the story of the Victoria Cross), 'The Story of Rolls Royce', numerous programmes in the 'People Talking' series, and a series called 'Challenge' where people with minority views met their critics.

In 1956 there were 1000 entries for the Northern Writers competition with the winner, 'The Life of Man', being broadcast in 1957. The winner broadcast in 1958 was 'Prisoner'. The station seemed to have an obsession about prisons in that year with a programme in the 'People Talking' about the subject, and a unit being allowed to film in Strangeways. Liverpool and Sheffield Playhouse companies, as well as those from York and Manchester Library Theatre, regularly presented plays. In 1957, the sound studios were modernised and magnetic tape recording facilities were increased so that only 25% of recordings were, by then, still made on acetate discs. It was a far cry from the Blattnerphone recording machine which recorded on thick metal ribbon. Editing of programmes was done by welding, and operators went out of the room when it was rewinding in case of a break, with the chance of injury from the coiled metal.

The BBC reaffirmed its faith in regional broadcasting in evidence to the Pilkington Committee of 1960, when the corporation stated, 'The BBC's regions, with their reserves of talent which can be enlisted and developed for network use . . . and which can provide (and already do) for the national audience regional entertainment the quality of which is indistinguishable from that of the metropolis'.

Certainly, in radio drama based at the Leeds studio, the North was doing great things. Alfred Bradley and Alan Ayckbourne encouraged new writers and hundreds of scripts were received each year at their offices. Three hundred scripts each year were submitted for the 'Northern Drift' which was included in the Sunday morning 'Talkabout' series. This was introduced by Brian Trueman and Peter Wheeler and edited by Herbert Smith. In 1979, the tradition of attracting local writers was continued with the programme 'Just After Noon' when 20,000 people responded to an invitation to submit material.

Plays produced in the region have won Italia Prizes, several Writers' Guild of Great Britain awards and have included the first radio play, 'The Daughter-in-Law', to be recorded entirely on location.

Four stories by Stan Barstow were broadcast before 'A Kind of Loving'; Keith Waterhouse wrote plays for Bradley before 'Billy Liar' brought him fame and Alan Plater took his first steps into professional writing with Bradley's help. Ayckbourne wrote plays himself for the station, and read hundreds of scripts by unknowns for inclusion in the 'Talkabout' programmes.

Stanley Williamson provided radio with several classic documentaries, one of which, 'Born To Trouble', was broadcast several times, and was eventually produced as a book and on record.

In several fields the north served both local and national audiences. Brian

Meeting to discuss a play from the Leeds studios. *Left to Right: Peter McKendrick, Joyce Palin, Brian Trueman, Herbert Smith, Trevor Hill, and Margaret Potter (author).*

Alfred Bradley.   **Alan Aykbourne.**

Two writers and producers who encouraged new writers in the 1950s and went on to have distinguished careers in their own fields.

New Broadcasting House, Oxford Road, Manchester.

The first radio production from Manchester's new headquarters in September 1975 was a reunion for Geoffrey Banks, Herbert Smith, Peter Wheeler, Billie Whitelaw, Brian Trueman, Philip Jenkinson and producer Trevor Hill.

Redhead was involved with several northern programmes and chaired the discussion programme 'A Word in Edgeways'; for Radio One John Wilcox produced numerous Radio One Club programmes; Harold Williamson and Michael Barton charmed youngsters into uninhibited speech in the 'Children Talking' series; Ray Short explored new techniques in religious broadcasting, and Don Mosey provided the national network with hundreds of outside broadcasts.

In the late seventies Manchester launched 'File On Four' for Radio Four, which has become an invaluable source of background information on current news items and has won awards in doing so. For Radio One Manchester provided the first regular programmes produced outside London with 'The Mike Read Show' and 'Discovatin'. More recently Read has had great success with his 'Pop Of The Form' quiz shows. On Radio Two Stuart Hall has enlivened Friday nights with a mixture of live and recorded music and the occasional chuckle. Light music from the region has included 'Listen to the Band', 'Rythm and Blues' and the long running 'The Organist Entertains'. Peter Pilbeam, involved in musical production from the region for forty years, recently retired.

Plays produced by Kay Patrick, Sue Hogg and Alfred Bradley have maintained the high standard of the region's plays winning prizes including the Giles Cooper Awards.

Regulars like 'Round Britain Quiz' and 'Gardeners' Question Time' never seem to date and could easily run into the next century. 'Trans-Atlantic Quiz' celebrated its 40th anniversary in 1984 whilst in 1987 saw forty years of 'Gardeners' Question Time' with a celebrity audience of gardeners.

'Cats Whiskers', a children's programme, specifically designed for the school holidays, proved sufficiently popular to restore the faith of some broadcasters that the spirit of 'Children's Hour' may not be really dead but merely metamorphosed.

Local Radio

As early as 1960, H. Carleton Greene, on a visit to Manchester, had said that the BBC would be interested in running local radio stations. In 1961, Postmaster General Bevins had been asked to agree to authorise a 'pilot' local radio scheme in Manchester, but it was not until 1966 that the Government's White Paper on Broadcasting gave the BBC the go ahead for an experimental Local Radio service.

Discussions were undertaken with several authorities for local sponsorship of the scheme. Manchester was initially in favour of providing some money for the scheme, but when Tories gained control of the city council they thought better of the idea.

Eight stations started the scheme. Leeds, though initially promised funds from the rates, was eventually refused by the Tory council, and as organisation of the station was underway, the BBC totally funded the scheme and surprisingly did not sue for the breaking of arrangements. The station opened with the irreverent line: 'Radio Leeds, it's a bloody waste of time'. This cynical humour pervaded many items in its first year, with its news bulletins being modestly entitled 'Leeds and the World', and the launch of the World Tune Gargling Contest. Air time was given over to local organisations and the station became increasingly involved with neighbourhood issues, some serious, some lighhearted.

After the experimental period, further stations were opened paid for from central funds. Manchester was one of the next group of stations to be opened in 1970, initially broadcasting on VHF only. The opening of this second group of stations coincided with, and was in part a consequence of, a total revision of the BBC's regional broadcasting scheme.

In July 1970, the three English regions of North, Midlands and South and West were disbanded. In their place were established eight English Television regions and three network production centres in Manchester, Birmingham and Bristol. The new order was layed out in a document written by Ian Trethowan, entitled 'Broadcasting in the Seventies'. The reorganisation caused much resentment in some quarters, but resulted in Manchester having a regional television role, a network television and radio production centre and a local radio station, which it was hoped would provide more community based programming.

The Local Station broadcasting on VHF found it difficult to attract listeners and struggled to establish an identity, as well as countering internal resentment from those formerly in regional radio. In 1974, transmission on the medium wave enabled a gradual increase in audience figures. The station had a 'middle of the road' musical policy but was fundamentally a speech based station. D.J.'s Dave Eastwood, Dave Eager, Ralph Elphinstone and The Baron, provided the music in the early days, whilst Sandra Chalmers, Alex Greenhalgh, Alan Sykes and colleagues presented news and discussions as well as manning the obligatory phone-in programmes. The station formed the Radio Manchester Chorale and was one of the few local stations to regularly present documentaries.

In 1975, the station moved to New Broadcasting House on Oxford Road, still preserving its own identity amidst the other activities of the region. Allan Shaw, the station manager, developed the community service aspect of the station and was rewarded by programmes of excellence by his news staff, and a growing concern for Manchester people from a dedicated workforce. The Late Night Line programmes, where people could call in for help on a wide range of subjects, have resulted in two changes in Acts of Parliament and brought comfort and concrete help for hundreds of listeners in the area.

Radio Manchester serves an audience of over three million and, unlike many other local stations with smaller population cover, has to encompass a range of smaller, quite distinct communities. To try to serve local needs, the station was the first to experiment with satellite stations and ringed Manchester with small studios for local interviews. A manned station was set up in Wigan and a recent experiment with sub-regional stations has proved very worthwhile.

In recent years the music output of the station has become more adventurous with a wide range of popular music from the sixties to the eighties attracting an increasingly younger audience. Specialist music programmes continue and have been to some extent strengthened in the evening, but the station remains strongly speech-based. 'Eastern Horizon' is Britain's first Chinese community magazine and along with 'I.N.I. Rule OK', 'Eastwards North Westwards' and 'Come into the Parlour' Radio Manchester has demonstrated an increasing provision for ethnic minority programming.

Three of the Radio Manchester Team:– Susie Mathis, Phil Sayer and Lindsay Leonard.

Stuart Whaley
Presenter on Radio Lancashire.

Debi Jones
Presenter on Radio Merseyside.

Kevin Fernihough
Presenter on Radio Cumbria.

———————— *Chapter Seven* ————————

A CENTRE OF EXCELLENCE

From almost the start of broadcasting, the BBC divided its operation into several distinct departments, and with minor changes, and the occasional movement of a programme from the responsibility of one department to that of another, these sections have remained. Sections such as the Talks Department, Outside Broadcasts, Music, Light Entertainment, News and others, provide a great diversity in entertainment and education. Several sections are mentioned elsewhere, but there are some areas which warrant a more detailed description because of their prominence in Manchester.

Serious Music

From the very first days of broadcasting, music, whether live or recorded, has made a major contribution to programming. Live music in the Trafford Park studio was sporadic and usually restricted to soloists or small ensembles. Outside broadcasts enabled the early technicians to add dance bands and cinema orchestras to their lists of entertainments. But it was not until Dan Godfrey arrived at Dickinson Street in 1923 that the Manchester Station could boast that it had its own orchestra.

Godfrey had a good musical pedigree with a great-grandfather who was a bandmaster in the Guards and a grandfather who took the first English military band to the United States. His father was Dan Godfrey who was then the Director of Music for Bournemouth Corporation. Dan Jnr. became Uncle Chuntie to children listeners. After a visit to the studio in December 1923, 'Ariel' of the Popular Wireless Weekly wrote a description of a musical broadcast from which the atmosphere of the place is evident. He wrote 'The 'Symphony Night' brought home to me forcibly, the great difficulties that Mr. Dan Godfrey and his staff work under. It made me realise that the success of the station is an even finer achievement than its most ardent admirers give it credit for.'

'The studio is roughly 33 ft by 14 ft, irregular in shape and mainly occupied by a huge grand piano. I was the first to enter and in so doing made, as I was soon to discover, a big blunder. I should have squeezed in last and remained by the door.

The 2ZY Trio. *Jessie Cormack, Sidney Wright and Leonard Hirsch.*

Dan Godfrey. *Station Director and Musical Director 1923–24.*

T. H. Morrison. *Succeeded Godfrey as Musical Director in 1924.*

The symphony orchestra assembled and as each one came in the thermometer raised a few degrees. In all 45, a full orchestra, assembled. Even with 25 there it was impossible for me to move or get out. Just when the walls were beginning to bulge, the conductor (Mr. Godfrey) arrived and took his place before the orchestra. I looked up as he stepped on the dais and received another shock. Do you think he was wearing evening dress and an uncomfortable stiff shirt? Not a bit of it. He was in Rugger jersey, the jersey of the Manchester Rugby Club.'

As well as the 2ZY Orchestra, Godfrey formed the Chorus, mainly made of singers from the Beecham and Halle Choruses, which he felt sounded better facing away from the microphone which was hung above their heads! There was also the 2ZY Quartet and the Radio Military Band under the baton of Harry Mortimer. Each member of the band was given £1 except Mortimer who, as conductor, was expected to perform without fee. The band usually performed on Sundays, the only day they were all free, with Mortimer playing clarinet as well as conducting.

The 2ZY Quartet consisted of Eric Fogg (piano), Don Hyden (violin), S. Wright (cello) and Pat Ryan (clarinet). These were four of the full Orchestra. Don Hyden had founded his quartet whilst a student at the Royal Manchester School of Music, and after Kenneth Wright had asked the college to provide a quartet for experimental broadcasts in 1922. Mr. Hyden went on to have a long career with the BBC until he retired from the BBC Northern Orchestra.

Other musical regulars included the O'Brien and other dance bands; baritone Harry Hopewell began his radio career at this time and was soon joined by Bella Redford, Lee Thistlethwaite and many others in evening recitals. There were so many requests from listeners for certain items, that sometimes whole evenings were given over to these 'Request Nights'. In one poll in 1924, the two most popular musical groups were the Don Hyden Quartet and the Garner Schofield Band. The Garner Schofield band first broadcast on 6 February, 1923, being almost certainly the first dance band to broadcast live in Britain.

T. H. Morrison succeeded Godfrey in May 1924 as Musical Director. Most of the orchestra belonged to the Halle Orchestra and had only a verbal agreement with the BBC that they should undertake four broadcasts each week for a fee of £4.4s. a week. It rapidly acquired a good reputation and a repertoire outside its original brief which was 'definitely for the purpose of playing light music for the Regional pool'.

In 1926 the Orchestra was renamed the Northern Wireless Orchestra and North Regional Director Edward Liveing, given an increased allowance for music, wished to increase its members and put the musicians under contract. National negotiations were proceeding with the Musicians Union at that time about rates of pay, holidays etc., but Manchester had the additional problem of the arrangement with the Halle. After pressure from Sir Hamilton Harty it was proposed that all those contracted to the BBC should be released for certain Halle Concerts. An agreement was signed in March 1928 and the orchestra members were given their first written contracts for one year. A Music Advisory Committee had been set up in 1927 which, as well as its artistic contributions, also formed a close link between the BBC and the local community.

The Northern Orchestra 1946. *Conductor Charles Groves, leader Reginald Stead at the Pavilion gardens, Buxton.*

A recent photograph of the BBC Philharmonic Orchestra at the Free Trade Hall, Manchester.

On 1 April, 1929, the number of musicians was increased to 28, but in 1930, because of the increased clarity of simultaneous broadcasting, Head Office made it known it intended to form a National Orchestra and provincial orchestras would not be needed. They suggested that Manchester reduced its numbers to an octet. Hamilton Harty was now worried that Halle players supported by BBC contracts, may not be able to be permanently employed by the Halle, and his orchestra would suffer. A compromise was reached whereby the BBC agreed to support a series of Promenade Concerts, which were musically successful but not so financially.

There was public outcry about the possible loss of what many considered to be the finest BBC orchestra, and annoyance at the refusal of the Halle to accept new proposals. In 1930, a deputation went to London and initially a further three months' contracts were issued to musicians, but the Northern Wireless Orchestra was finally reduced to a nonet in 1931 and known as the Northern Studio Orchestra. After a few turbulent years with the Halle and Liverpool Philharmonic, the BBC decided to increase regional status, and in 1934 a new arrangement was made with the Halle. A new orchestra of 35 was formed to be called the BBC Northern Orchestra.

When Morrison retired he was succeeded by Foster Clarke, and later by Gideon Fagan. Sir Thomas Beecham, Sir Hamilton Harty, Sir Adrian Boult, John Barbirolli, Dr. Malcolm Sargent, Leslie Heward and Julius Harrison, all took turns with the baton until, in 1944, Charles Groves was appointed permanent conductor. In that year the numbers were increased to 43, and in 1945 to 50. Groves widened the repertoire still further. He said in 1949 that 'The repertoire embraces the whole of symphonic music'. In 1954, the numbers were again increased and the 57 musicians could rightly be described as a symphony orchestra. In the same year the BBC Northern Singers were formed under the direction of Stephen Wilkinson. The ensemble's repertoire soon encompassed folk song, madrigal, cantata and opera. Their reputation also grew, being described by one critic as having 'a kind of corporate virtuosity'.

By 1960, the orchestra was accepted as the corporation's second symphony orchestra. Many public concerts were given, and by 1960 it had 60 players. In that year it gave its first promenade concert.

By 1964, the North Region Music Department was responsible for 400 programmes each year. The Orchestra played in such programmes as 'Concert Hour', 'Music of the Masters', 'Music To Remember' and the 'Northern Proms'. It also played in musical biography programmes, and a series of Operas, and provided film music for programmes like 'The Horse' and 'The Great War'.

A noteable member of the orchestra was leader Reginald Stead, who as early as 1925, had broadcast for the BBC in a concert party. He joined the orchestra in the mid 1940's, giving many years devoted service to music in the North.

Concerts by other northern orchestras were broadcast; choral societies, children's choirs and the BBC Northern Singers provided voices for operas, religious programmes and numerous concerts; there were chamber music concerts, solo recitals and brass band programmes. The department also initiated the programmes by Max Jaffa, from Scarborough.

The BBC Northern Orchestra became known as the BBC Northern Symphony Orchestra in 1967, having 70 musicians by then. In 1969, Gerald McDonald, Head

Jack Hardy's Little Orchestra. *At the microphone are Doris Gambell and Robert Irwin.*

The Northern Variety Orchestra 1954, conducted by Alyn Ainsworth.

of Music in the North, arranged for the Orchestra to take its first ever trip abroad, which was an outstanding success. Further tours followed including those to Hong Kong and, in 1983, behind the Iron Curtain to Bulgaria.

In 1982, the Orchestra was renamed the BBC Philharmonic Orchestra with a complement of 89 musicians. Its international reputation was further enhanced by major European tours in 1983 and 1984.

Milton Hall was the Orchestra's home for many years, but with the construction of New Broadcasting House, and the completion of Studio 7, it was given a new home in 1980, the year Edward Downes became Principal Conductor.

The orchestra now has a thriving Philharmonic Club of enthusiastic supporters and the club members were delighted recently to be given the opportunity to present the prizes in the 'Young Musician of the Year' competition.

Light Music

For light and popular music in the 1930's, Manchester relied heavily on local bands such as Jack Hardy's Little Orchestra, Toni and his North Pier Orchestra, and Richard Valery and his Piccadilly Orchestra. Things changed somewhat when Ray Martin brought his London based band to Manchester for regular broadcasts. His was a dance band with strings and brought more modern music to the station. As well as playing dance music they also accompanied variety programmes but were expensive to transport regularly from London. Martin was eventually asked to form an orchestra using northern musicians, and Johnny Roadhouse was asked to round up a few suitable musicians. These became part of the orchestra, which by 1950 consisted of 5 brass, 5 saxophones, 4 rhythm, 12 violins and a harp, each being paid £2.6s. a performance.

Bowker Andrews was determined to have an in-house band – 'our own Northern Variety Orchestra'. Ray Martin left as he presumably wished to control his own band, and he took with him his library of arrangements. Vilem Tausky, who was more at home on a classical podium than with a variety orchestra, took charge, and with arrangements written by a young Bolton lad, he began the N.V.O.. When Tausky left, another conductor was proving hard to find until the young arranger from Bolton, Alyn Ainsworth, considered he could do as well as anyone else. Producer Ronnie Taylor gave him a trial, and using his own familiar arrangements, became a hit with listeners and musicians alike. Dedicated to the job, he would sit up till all hours listening to American broadcasts so that he could adapt their arrangements for the Northern Orchestra, and he put the band on the map with lively, modern arrangements and lighthearted, humorous programmes like 'Make Way For Music'. The humour was often supplied by the sometimes outspoken announcer, Roger Moffat. After announcing that the band was to play 'I Can't Tell A Waltz from a Tango', the orchestra, having had no rehearsal and with a mix up of music, eventually came to a grinding halt. Moffat, unflappable, remarked that it just proved that they couldn't tell a waltz from a tango and went on to the next item. Such catastrophies were a very rare occurrence and the band set a new standard. Using the N.V.O. as an example of modern trends, other regional bands were given the ultimatum:– 'Get modern or get out'.

The Argyle Theatre, Birkenhead.
Without headphones, Victor Smythe announcing the acts.

DON'T TINKER ABOUT! Have YOUR set adjusted by an expert in time for the the next Broadcast from the **ARGYLE**, Birkenhead, on

Combined concerts with the BBC Northern Orchestra were arranged when works by Dankworth, Seiber, Gershwin and specially commissioned pieces were played.

The orchestra also provided incidental music for programmes such as 'The Clitheroe Kid' and 'Variety Fanfare', as well as having its own shows. Economies eventually forced the orchestra to drop the strings and it became The Northern Dance Orchestra, and Jimmy Leach on the organ joined to try and make up for the lost strings. When Ainsworth left for London, Bernard Herrmann, who had been leading a small section of the orchestra in programmes, seemed an automatic choice for the conductor's position. Meticulous and accurate with a sense of fun, he made the N.D.O. a household name with numerous 'pop' and variety shows featuring singers Les Howard and Sheila Buxton. Various musicians of the band were grouped to form smaller units, some like the 'Trad Lads' becoming very popular.

Visiting the Playhouse Theatre when the band was playing, Barney Colehan remarked on the casual dress and relaxed atmosphere, and kept this style when he televised the orchestra in the television version of 'Make Way for Music'. The band was to make numerous television appearances in the 1960's.

In 1976, there was another format change and the Northern Radio Orchestra came into being with new conductor Neil Richardson. Economies and changing trends in music, led in 1981 to the disbanding of the staff orchestra and all modern music is now on a freelance basis.

Variety

From the days at Trafford Park and Dickinson Street, Victor Smythe had taken it upon himself to organise variety and light entertainment for the station, and it was he who, in 1931, arranged to broadcast a variety show from the Argyle Theatre, Birkenhead. The proprietor, Mr. D. J. Clarke was keen on broadcasting and, unlike other theatre impresarios, wanted close involvement with wireless. He often engaged talent he had heard on the wireless, and for a six month trial period agreed to book artists for broadcasts, from the theatre. The arrangement worked so well that three acts were still being booked for each performance in summer 1933. By that time, Stoll theatres were also allowing broadcasts from their establishments in Halifax, Huddersfield, Chester, York and Manchester.

Throughout the thirties and forties, Victor Smythe produced hundreds of outside broadcast variety programmes from resorts. In 1942, for example, he organised some 59 from Northern theatres, and 52 in the 'Works Wonders' series of factory concerts.

'Northern Music Hall' became a regular weekly feature but was criticized in a report produced by Percy Edgar (Midland Station Director), as were other variety programmes from the regions, as being below standard. John Watt in London argued that 'Northern Music Hall' was giving a local audience the entertainment it wanted, not what Head Office thought they should have. Certainly the long run of the programme seemed to disprove its critics. It celebrated its 1000th edition in February, 1947.

The Radio Times for 30 May, 1930, announced a programme 'Famous Northern Resorts: Blackpool', which was opened by a special recital by R. H. Dixon at the

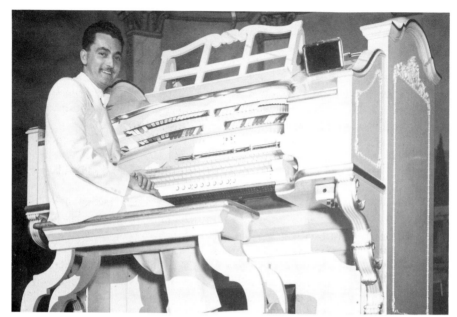

Mr. Blackpool to holiday makers and radio listeners alike – *Reginald Dixon at the Wurlitzer organ of the Tower Ballroom, Blackpool.*

'Over The Garden Wall'. *Norman Evans as Fanny, talking to Betty Jumel as Betty the neighbour.*

organ of the Tower Ballroom. Reginald Dixon, who became Mr. Blackpool to holidaymakers and radio listeners, had begun a long series of broadcasts from the tower. Utilising the numerous entertainers at northern resorts, the North Region broadcast regularly from Blackpool, Morecambe and other seaside venues. That original organ played by Dixon in the tower was moved to the Winter Gardens in 1935, and in 1970 was fitted, by the original company, in the BBC's own Playhouse Theatre. It was the acquisition of the Playhouse Theatre which allowed more scope in light entertainment for the region.

The Playhouse Theatre was built in Hulme by William Henry Broadhead, who built 15 theatres in Manchester, and was opened in October, 1902. It was purchased by the BBC in 1955, some variety shows being previously recorded at the Playhouse's sister theatre next door, the Hulme Hippodrome.

The north has always been a rich source of comedians and several of them have performed particularly well on radio. Variety Fanfare and Northern Variety Parade, produced on different occasions by Bowker Andrews, Eric Miller, Ronnie Taylor, John Ammonds, Geoff Lawrence and James Casey, were able to tap into this talent. These high speed series were a springboard for many up and coming artists to be heard nationally. Ken Platt, Morecambe and Wise, Ken Dodd, Bob Monkhouse as well as old favourites like Norman Evans and Albert Modley, were included in the shows.

Variety Fanfare was able to achieve a uniquely slick presentation by the clever use of the singing group 'The Kordites' who sang short musical links between acts. These, written by Ronnie Taylor, often had cryptic clues to the identity of the next artist. For example for Harry Bailey:—

'Gags in vogue, and Irish brogue,
We're joking, provoking,
A laughter beano, that's why we know,
His gags will carry, we're wild about Harry.'

One of Bowker Andrews' ambitions in beginning 'Variety Fanfare' was to give new talent a start on radio. Al Read became a household name through the programme and Ken Platt was given his first chance on the show. Ronnie Taylor found Platt serving behind the counter in a grocer's shop in Leigh. He was given an audition the same night and within a fortnight he was on 'Variety Fanfare'. Developing his catchphrases of 'I won't take me coat off, I'm not stopping' and 'Daft as a brush' he went on to have his own shows.

Morecambe and Wise were given their very first radio series in Manchester with a show called 'You're Only Young Once' or 'YOYO'. Peter Goodwright was given his first radio break on the same show.

Norman Evans was one of the first to have his own series of shows with 'Over the Garden Wall'. He had been spotted by Gracie Fields doing his comedy routines in a charity show in Rochdale and she suggested he should turn professional. This he did in the mid-thirties, and his 'Garden Wall' and dentist sketches were topping the bill within three years. For his radio shows, he insisted on dressing in character and after the shows would often take the cast in a coach for a meal. Evans starred in the live television shows from the Playhouse called 'Make Yourself at Home'.

James Casey, writing for Evans, invented a young upstart child character who was used by Ronnie Taylor in a programme called 'The Mayor's Parlour' starring Jimmy James. The child was played by Jimmy Clitheroe who went on to do his own series called 'Call Boy'. In May, 1958, 'The Clitheroe Kid' was born. It ran for fourteen years and 279 programmes, drawing a peak listening audience of ten-and-half million. James Casey's scripts were not sophisticated but he and Clitheroe were able to find an authenticity in the situations, and young and old alike could identify with the cheeky youngster's antics.

Jimmy James' radio programmes had a shaky start and, though popular, James never achieved the outstanding success he had as a theatre comic. Frank Randle too, never emulated his stage success on the wireless.

Dave Morris's 'Club Night' was a great favourite in the north in the mid-fifties. Morris had been badly gassed in the First World War. His health suffered since then and gave rise to, amongst other things, very poor sight. This became so bad that he could not read scripts and all shows therefore, had to be well rehearsed. On one occasion when the live show was being broadcast from a working men's club in Clayton, there was a power failure just before the beginning of the show which lasted the whole programme. Morris, script perfect, was alright while the rest rushed around for torches and matches. The show always contained the famous question from Fred Ferris as the Wacker, 'As 'e bin in?', but Morris would not tell the rest of the cast his pay-off gag until they heard it, as did the audience, at the end of the show. The BBC was asked by one Sheffield company if the programme could be put on half an hour later as none of their employees wanted to work overtime the night of the show – such was its popularity.

Ronnie Taylor produced and wrote the Al Read Shows, starring the uniquely talented Al Read. Though limited in theatrical expertise, he was ideal for radio. The verbal pictures of the one-way telephone conversation 'J–j–j–just a minute'; the drunk 'We've supped some stuff tonight!', and the husband home from the office or a night out, 'That's the wife from the kitchen' are indelible memories.

Like many others, Al's show was repeated, having been recorded. One such recording was sent off, by mistake, to the Overseas Service on the day it was to be repeated. Engineers, discovering this error, drove off to London Road Station in the hope of finding the missing acetate disc. It was found in a pile of parcels and eventually released by the railway authority after much argument. With only minutes to spare, the recording arrived at Broadcasting House in Piccadilly and was broadcast. The crew smiled when they heard Al make his opening remarks, 'Nobody will know the trouble I've had to get here!'.

'Such is life;
Life is what you make it.
Such is life;
Show them you can take it
On the chin
With a grin.
When Mr. Blue comes around
Don't let him in . . . '

The Clitheroe Kid – *Jimmy Clitheroe with Diana Day (Susan), Peter Sinclair (Grandad), Leonard Williams (Theodore Claythorpe) and Patricia Burke (Mother).*

Al Read on stage at the Playhouse presenting the 'Al Read Show' 1955.

Exterior and interior photographs of the Playhouse Theatre. *The home of radio and television variety in the North for thirty years.*

Half hour radio comedy programmes from northern comics like Ken Dodd, Mike Yarwood, Les Dawson and Roy Castle, have continued the tradition, but without the mass audiences of their forerunners, as listeners became viewers. Eli Woods and Roy Castle, both one-time stooges for Jimmy James, were heard regularly together in 'Castle's On The Air'; 'Listen to Les' offered Les Dawson the opportunity, amongst other things, to insult his mother-in-law, and shows like 'The Show With Ten Legs' allowed Liverpool script-writer Eddie Braben to perform some of his own lines. The versatile Grumbleweeds achieved far greater fame than the years of touring northern clubs could ever have given them when they were given their own radio programme in the seventies.

It was a sad night on June 15, 1986, when the last show from the Playhouse was recorded. Home of radio and television variety for over thirty years, the theatre is now 'no longer able to meet today's broadcasting needs'. Many performers with special memories of the theatre took part, including The Beverley Sisters, Les Dawson, Peter Goodwright, The Grumbleweeds and David Hamilton who made his radio debut at the theatre. Les Dawson, who was given his chance on radio by James Casey, summed up everyones' feelings when he said 'It's the atmosphere that makes the Playhouse so special. You cannot buy it, you cannot build or replace it.'

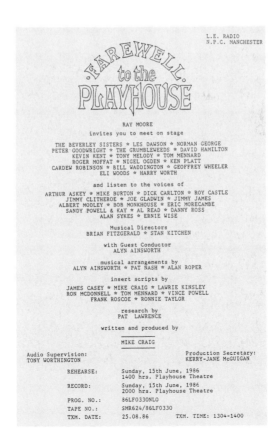

Chapter Eight

TELEVISION

In 1936, the BBC initiated the first regular television service. It was hampered by the decision of the Selsdon Committee to allow both the Baird and EMI–Marconi systems to be used alternately, but by 1937, the Baird system was dropped. The service was suspended during the war but resumed in 1946 serving the London area. The North had little to do with early television development, although the Yorkshire Weekly Post Illustrated had reported in 1930 that Baird was to operate television tests in the North Region using the Moorside Edge Transmitter. This never materialised however.

It was not until the Holme Moss transmitter was opened in October 1951 by Lord Simon of Wythenshawe that northerners had a television service. On the opening night, the ceremony at the Town Hall was broadcast, followed by variety from Leeds, and on successive nights a version of 'Have A Go' from Blackpool and a televised church service from Leeds.

Holme Moss was built high in the Pennines with a 750 ft mast which was 1,700 ft above sea level. It was to serve a population of 13 million and was constructed to resist the severe weather conditions of the area with an ability to withstand winds of 120 mph. Manchester was designated the main national television programme distribution centre, connected visually to London via Birmingham by coaxial cable. The sound component was connected by Post Office 'music' lines.

The region had already been supplying London with film, mainly for news programmes, using freelance cameramen, but with the opening of Holme Moss, the region could offer 'live' outside broadcasts. In 1952, the region undertook coverage of numerous sporting events including boxing from Liverpool and the Rugby League Final, as well as the first television appearance of Gerald Iles in a programme from Belle Vue Zoo for Children's Television. An outside broadcast unit consisted of control vehicle with three cameras and about fourteen staff involved in its running. The capital cost was about £65,000 with running costs of about £100,000 per annum. It was not until 1955 that the region received its own permanent unit.

On 30 September, 1957, the region started its own television news service with 'News of the North' from the Dickenson Road studio read by Tom Naisby, Philip

The first televised variety show from the North of England in 1951. *Barney Colehan, second left, produced the show with, as you see, a multitude of famous names.*

Randal Herley

Tom Naisby

Outside broadcast van at the Rydal Sheep Dog Trials in 1929.

The North Region 'Roving Eye' located on a Humber Super Snipe. *The car pulled its own petrol electric generator and could be used over a maximum range of half a mile. March 1961.*

Dobson, Roger Moffat and Randal Herley. There was often a mad dash from Broadcasting House by taxi for the newsreaders. Great efforts were made to illustrate the news, but initially there were usually only a couple of film items and a few 'stills'. In December, 1959, a news studio was brought into use at Broadcasting House, Piccadilly, when the old boardroom and library were converted, and new freelance announcers arrived. The new studio had a vision and sound control room, interview area and two new Vidicon cameras.

There was a reorganisation of regional television in 1962 with each region being allowed 25 minutes news time Monday to Friday and 'North at Six' was launched. Experiments by Don Haworth with a more conversational style of news format allowed Colin Welland, with black shirt and no tie, to attempt a more 'laid back' approach. This caused such controversy and Welland left for 'Z Cars' and Academy Awards.

The Outside Broadcast Department covered all sports in the region as well as civic functions, religious, theatrical and musical items outside the studio. Producers had to be masters of all trades, but some began to specialise in their own particular interests. Ray Lakeland along with the individual, but much impersonated, style of Eddie Waring as commentator, was principally responsible for giving Rugby League national fame. Golf, bowling, boxing, racing and even 'Come Dancing' were also covered by the same team.

The Grand National was always a special event in the sports calendar and has been covered on numerous occasions by northern cameras. However, the standard O.B. van with camera perched on top, had difficulty in keeping pace with the horses. A car was specially converted to take a camera, which, being nearer to the ground, also gave a more dramatic picture. Because of the space restriction in the car, the smallest cameraman in Manchester, Don McKay, was given the job and captured exciting shots of the race.

As techniques and audiences became more sophisticated, producers began to specialise in their own sports or entertainments. Nick Hunter, initially gaining experience on a variety of broadcasts, became renowned for his coverage of cricket and snooker. Hunter and his colleagues have been responsible for the tremendous popularity of snooker, and more recently darts. Now the Manchester cameras cover the whole country for their specialist sports.

The World Snooker final of 1985, between Dennis Taylor and Steve Davies, was viewed by 18,500,000 people, and this until the early hours of the morning. This was the highest viewing figure ever achieved for BBC2 and the highest for any programme in Britain after midnight. The BBC, at a loss as to how to honour the two contestants, made them honorary members of the BBC.

Weather always plays an important part in all outside broadcasts and many is the time that the whole entourage has had to pack up and speed to another venue. Sometimes the weather can bring amusement as in the 'to camera' assessment of the day's cricket by Messrs. West and Benaud when the umbrella held by West, gradually moved from over both commentators to cover West only. The viewers witnessed the rain hitting West's brolly and cascading directly into Benaud's collar. Today, commentary staff have the luxury of a roof, in most cases.

Radio Times of 18 March, 1960, announcing the first televised Grand National.

Danny La Rue steps back into the Gay 90's for 'The Good Old Days'. April 1970.

In 1947, Mancunian Films had bought the church in Dickenson Road, which housed the Rusholme Wesleyan Sunday School, and converted it into a film studio. There they produced dozens of features starring Frank Randle, Sandy Powell, Tessie O'Shea, Jimmy James and others. The premises were acquired by the BBC in 1954 to be used as a television studio. The dressing rooms still had signs on the doors for Randle and Diana Dors when the BBC staff moved in. It was the first premises to be used for television outside London, but was soon closed for refurbishment and reopened in April, 1956. The Manchester studios thus had only begun to gain experience in studio television production, when Granada Television began broadcasting in May, 1956. It was the possibility that Sidney Bernstein of Granada might be interested in the Dickenson Road premises, that stimulated the BBC to make an early bid. The studios were operated for many years on a drive-in basis, where a mobile control room was used in order to allow greatest possible use of the restricted studio space.

By 1956, the north was making 650 annual contributions, mainly as outside broadcasts, to the national network, including 200 major programmes. Many of the ideas for popular entertainment programmes over the first twenty-seven years of television in the North, have been thought of and developed in a small room in Leeds where Barney Colehan, and his long serving secretary Dorothy Bickerdike, found successful formulae on numerous occasions. After producing 'Have A Go' for six years, and with Pickles threatening to leave the programme, Colehan thought the time had come to move and was able to get an attachment to London in television. After twelve months, he became the first television producer employed by the North Region, Derek Burrell Davies having been seconded earlier from London. It was Davies who, whilst producing a circus, had one of the early experiences with the unpredictability of animals. During the time the ring was being changed between acts, Davies had the idea to have a small area set aside for novelty acts to fill in time. One such act was a dog which unfortunately had been kept in its box for some time before being let out to perform. The dog took the opportunity to relieve itself and the single camera watched its performance for a good two minutes.

One of Colehan's early ideas was to produce 'The Story of Music Hall', which used some members of the audience dressed in different period costume watching acts from Victorian and Edwardian periods. Deryck Guyler told the story as the 'spirit of the theatre' and the programme was brought up-to-date with Stan Stennett and Joan Turner as current performers. London liked the programme and asked for more. Colehan decided the Edwardian setting was preferable and so began 'The Good Old Days'. Soon artists were eager to appear on the programme as audiences were shown another facet of their skills, and audiences too clammered to dress up in costume with, at one time, a waiting list of 20,000. The show had a perfect setting in the City Varieties in Leeds. With Leonard Sachs becoming the ebullient chairman and countless novelty and speciality acts, as well as stars of the day, the programme ran for thirty years — a world record.

Following the success of 'Top Town' on radio, where amateurs such as Norman Collier and David Whitfield were first heard by the general public, Colehan moved the idea to television. This was the first programme to open the refurbished Dickenson

Road studios. This competition between different towns was seen by visitors from French television who wanted to try the idea themselves, but due to their difficulties with travelling and insufficient talent, they decided on a competition with games. French television asked Colehan if he was interested in seeing the idea with a view to possible international competition, so Colehan and Robin Scott, from London, went to France and saw the programme. The outcome was 'It's A Knockout' which began on Morecambe sands one Sunday in 1966. It was introduced by Ted Ray and Charlie Chester, with Macdonald Hobley on the scoreboard and Eddie Waring as referee. Competition with the French and Dutch followed in 'Jeux Sans Frontieres' which attracted 16–17 million viewers in its first year. There were those who thought that this type of show was a little beneath the BBC but a glance at the ratings persuaded them to keep it running for many years.

David Vine became presenter (with the help of Eddie Waring), but when the programme clashed with another popular show from the North, 'A Question of Sport', on which he was questionmaster, he was replaced by Stuart Hall. Hall's infectious laugh and ebullient personality helped to continue the programme's popularity. The programme production was unique in that the whole team and equipment travelled the country to each venue. Normally the producer would use cameras and other equipment from the area of the transmission, but an exception was made in this case because of the complexity of the programmes.

Two pilot programmes were viewed by Head of Light Entertainment, Eric Mashwitz and Tom Sloan, then his assistant, on two consecutive days in the North. One featured a tartan haired DJ who brought his own equipment and friends into the studio for a show called 'Teen and Twenty Club'. The other was a band show with a more relaxed and sophisticated presentation called 'Make Way For Music'. The visitors were more struck with the second programme, but said that if the first was to be used they could not possibly use the weird presenter. Six months later, Johnny Stewart came up from London to take up that idea in 'Top of the Pops' and the first presenter was that weird DJ, Jimmy Savile, whose fame had rapidly grown. The show was produced at Dickenson Road for many years until it was moved south in 1965. It followed other programmes featuring Harry Worth and Val Doonican which, once established in the North, moved to be produced in London.

In 'Make Way For Music' Colehan, who enjoyed the relaxed, informal air of the radio programmes, endeavoured to bring the informality and humour of rehearsals to the screen. Roger Moffatt, announcer of the show, took receipt one day of a wig for Sheila Buxton. To add some of his own brand of humour to the show, Moffatt on this occasion went to Platt Fields to gather a sack or two of leaves, which he sprinkled over Miss Buxton as she sang 'Falling Leaves'. After the song, remembering the wig, he brushed the leaves from Sheila's hair with a deliberate force that dislodged the wig in full view of the audience.

Jan and Vlasda Dalibor were Czechoslovaks who had settled in Yorkshire in 1948. Jan Dalibor had been a professor of sculpture in Czechoslovakia and as a refugee, had been forced to go into mining in Yorkshire. Jan was introduced to Colehan by a mutual friend, Jack Tomelty, and demonstrated the puppets he had carved in a programme called 'Let's Make A Date' which was introduced by Brian Reese. A spot

Barney Colehan with the Top Town Trophy, 1956.

Alyn Ainsworth and Sheila Buxton on the set of 'Little Miss Music', December 1959.

Sooty. *Probably the most popular glove puppet in Britain for over thirty years. Here with Harry Corbett in 1955.*

Val Doonican outside the Dickenson Road Studios where his early television shows were produced until his move to London. *A plaque has been sited where the studios, now demolished, once stood.*

on 'It's Up To You' in 1956, allowed the couple to demonstrate their puppetry skills and Pinky and Perky soon became household names, miming to popular records.

A senior cameraman at Dickenson Road was Stan Parkinson who took the opportunity to go into production and went on to introduce Ken Dodd's Diddymen to the television as well as many Ray Allen shows. Both he and Trevor Hill produced the Pinky and Perky shows.

Trevor Hill began his broadcasting career as effects boy on ITMA and became one of the most experienced producers in the North, especially on children's programmes. With the coming of television he spent some time in the mid 1950's working for Freda Lingstrom, Head of Children's Television, at Lime Grove and returned to Manchester determined to offer quality children's television programmes from the north. He contacted Wilfred Pickles in the hope that he would host a regular programme. Hill also wanted to use children as presenters in the successful way Northern Children's Hour had used them. Judith Chalmers took time off school for her television audition and got the job along with Pickles, introducing 'Children's Television Club' which had a similar format as Blue Peter was to have.

It was Hill too, who for years produced another puppet programme in Manchester. Sooty, the glove puppet, was the brainchild of Bradford businessman Harry Corbett, who gave an impish personality to a doll he bought on holiday in Blackpool. Corbett phoned Barney Colehan one day to tell him of his new magic act using his glove puppet and Colehan was persuaded to view the act and immediately phoned Derek Burrell Davies who had seen more puppet acts than he cared to remember. However, another audition was held for him and Sooty was on television within hours.

Sooty was only able to whisper to his stooge, Corbett, who had to interpret and he uttered such phrases as 'Izzy wizzy, let's get busy – magic', when performing his tricks. It was also Corbett who took beatings with hammers and dowsings from water pistols, only to leave us with a plaintive, 'Bye bye everybody, bye bye'.

The region began to make new types of programmes and Denis Mitchell was able to transfer his unique sound documentaries to television with the help of Roy Harris. Notable programmes were 'In Prison' and 'Morning in the Streets' which won an Italia Prize. Stanley Williamson produced excellent film documentaries such as 'Waters of the Irwell' and 'Pastures in High Places'. Don Haworth continued this excellent tradition with films based on northern themes, winning international acclaim. Haworth made his mark as a playwright also, with plays broadcast on Radio 3. The reputation of the region for drama was enhanced by television plays such as 'When We Are Married', 'Love on the Dole', 'A Smashing Day' and many more. Northern playwrights were encouraged by competitions for both radio and television.

'Fish Is The Living' was the first colour documentary from the north. In 1968, Jack Saltman told the tale of a trip of a trawler from Hull with all its excitement and danger. The story of the air disaster in the same year, when a plane crashed in Stockport, was told by Barry Bevins and the Manchester Newsroom team. The incident was fully investigated initially for northern viewers, but the quality of the programme warranted national coverage. The north also has provided many fine documentaries and investigative discussion programmes like the 'Brass Tacks' series.

More light-hearted discussion has been provided by The Russell Harty programmes from Manchester studios.

The facilities for broadcasting in Manchester have always been inadequate for the talents and imagination of those wishing to broadcast. From the earliest days, technicians and producers have 'made do', and as more space was required new annexes were added so that, by the mid-sixties, some thirteen different premises were being used by the corporation in the city. Piccadilly, the Playhouse, Dickenson Road, Milton and Houldsworth Halls afforded studios. The outside broadcast department with the film unit formerly operated from a converted church in Plymouth Grove and became housed on Stockport Road, Levenshulme. Administration was squeezed out of Broadcasting House into Peter House in St. Peter's Square and the film processing laboratory was in Lever Street. The station was spread inefficiently throughout the city. Something needed to be done.

As early as 1953, the BBC had formulated plans to create a new television and radio headquarters and an initial site was purchased. Requirements for production steadily increased and it was soon realised that this site, opposite Platt Fields, would be far too small. It was Manchester City Council who suggested the site in All Saints and purchased the properties in the area after lengthy negotiations. Detailed planning began in 1967 and culminated with phase one of the development being completed in 1975. Staff moved from Piccadilly, Peter House and outside broadcasts in July 1975.

This initial phase provided a general-purpose television studio with a scenery and property store, artists facilities, workshops, a film processing area and a large base for the outside broadcast units' vehicles. Radio studios for drama and a self-contained area for Radio Manchester, as well as a central technical area, control suite, offices, restaurant and car park, at last brought most of the staff together under one roof.

The Orchestra was still based in Milton Hall until phase two provided them with a magnificent concert studio. Acoustic design had come a long way from the sailcloth hung on the walls of 2ZY. The design involved the construction of a model studio, analysis of absorbent surfaces, detailed reverberation measurement and numerous subjective tests before the work was complete. The result was one of the finest orchestral studios in Europe. Phase three involved the addition of facilities for regional television and at last all departments came together in a purpose-built unit.

In the late 1970's and early 1980's, television output increased dramatically. There were some industrial relations problems and financial restrictions, and staff losses especially affected outside broadcasts. Nevertheless, by 1984 the Network centre was producing, on average, almost a programme each day of the year. 'Screen Test', 'The Movie Quiz', which developed into 'Film Buff of the Year' and the increasingly popular 'A Question of Sport', have been three quiz programmes from the region. 'A Question of Sport' had the unique honour of being the first quiz show to have the participation of a member of the Royal Family when Princess Anne took part in the 200th edition. This was excellent television, somewhat enhanced by Emlyn Hughes' gaff on a previous programme when he failed to recognise the Princess from a

David Jacobs comperes this show and bare-footed Sandy Shaw entertains an audience a little more reserved than that of today's shows.

Pinky and Perky. *After their first break on television in Manchester they went on to appear on the London Palladium and in New York on the Ed Sullivan Show.*

Stuart Hall enjoying himself, as usual, introducing another crazy game on 'It's A Knockout'.

Hall again in the slightly more placid atmosphere of the 'Northwest Tonight' studio with fellow presenter John Mundy.

A Question of Sport. *Emlyn Hughes, David Coleman and Bill Beaumont.*

The Open Air regulars. *Eamonn Holmes, Bob Wellings and Pattie Coldwell.*

'No Limits'. *Tony Baker and Jenny Powell on either side of the ubiquitous Johnathan King.*

photograph, even incorrectly identifying her gender!

Contributions to factual series like 'Look Stranger' and 'Blue Peter Specials' have come from the region as well as the provision of its own regular series 'Living on the Land' and 'A Taste of Britain' by Ian Nairn and John Noakes.

Russell Harty and, more recently, Alan Whicker, have presented chat shows and Harty took a leaf out of Whicker's book by touring European Cities and Hollywood.

The current affairs department is second only to London on its output with 'Brass Tacks' on television and the award winning 'File on Four' on radio, being perhaps the most notable programmes. Documentaries have recently included the magnificent 'Great Railway Journeys of the World', Michael Wood's 'In search of the Trojan War' and a series about crucial points in people's lives entitled 'Moment of Truth'.

Mike Harding, Rod Hull with Emu, and Hinge and Bracket in 'Dear Ladies', have provided comedy from the region, and the ending of 'The Good Old Days' enabled Roy Hudd to take his own nostalgic voyage into music hall with 'Halls of Fame'. A major contribution to children's broadcasting has been 'The Saturday Picture Show' as well as 'Stopwatch' and 'Fax', the latter gaining over 7 million regular viewers. Rock and pop output from the region has also increased notably with 'No Limits', a rock magazine which began in 1986 and is now one of the most popular such programmes on British television.

With an increasing interest in daytime television Manchester has taken up the challenge in a big way with the 'Open Air' series of daily programmes. The show began in October 1986 and all concerned were soon being congratulated, not only for the programmes quality, but also on its high audience ratings. Under the co-ordination of Peter Ridsdale Scott, the North is in the forefront of encouraging independent producers and several projects are currently being undertaken.

Almost concurrent with the arrival of Hugh Williams as Head of Broadcasting, the region underwent a major change. 1986 has seen the re-establishment of a new English Regional structure, with Manchester the centre of the North West Region. The new structure has been designed to bring together network radio, regional television and the local radio stations in the North West under one management. The expansion of the region has been followed by increased news coverage in Cumbria with refurbished television facilities based in Cumbria and Merseyside. The News Department has also demonstrated its ability to produce compelling 'specials' some at short notice.

The new structure will, hopefully, enable northern broadcasters to continue the high standards which have in the past created a broadcasting heritage, of which the north can be justly proud.

Index

Other titles from Willow Publishing

Looking Back at Altrincham
Basil Morrison

Looking Back at Knutsford
K Goodchild, P Ikin, J Leach

Looking Back at Northenden
Derick Deakin

Looking Back at Rusholme & Fallowfield
Peter Helm & Gay Sussex

Looking Back at Sale
Vivien Hainsworth

Looking Back at Timperley
Hazel Pryor

Looking Back at Wilmslow
Morris Garratt

Old Manchester Illustrated
Chris Makepeace

Looking Back at Wythenshawe
Jean Greatorex & Sheila Clarke

Bollin Valley
Joan French

Walks Around Manchester
Ramblers' Association

The Lost Rivers of Manchester
Geoffrey Ashworth

Looking Back at Chorlton
John Lloyd

Looking Back at Levenshulme & Burnage
Peter Helm, Gay Sussex & Andrew Brown

Trafford Childhood
Frances Lennon

Willow
PUBLISHING

Willow Cottage, 36 Moss Lane, Timperley,
Altrincham, Cheshire, WA15 6SZ.